ON
THE AINDRA SCHOOL OF SANSKRIT GRAMMARIANS

ON
THE AINDRA SCHOOL OF SANSKRIT GRAMMARIANS

THEIR PLACE IN THE SANSKRIT AND SUBORDINATE LITERATURES

BY

A. C. BURNELL

GYAN

Published by

GYAN

Gyan Publishing House
5, Ansari Road
Daryaganj, New Delhi-110002
Phone: 011-47034999, 9811692060
E-mail: books@gyanbooks.com

Distribution Network
gyanbooks.com
India, USA, Canada, UK, Australia

ISBN: 978-93-6280-562-1 (HB)
First Published, 1875

2nd Impression 2024

Printed at: Gyan Press, Delhi.

ON THE AINDRA SCHOOL OF SANSKRIT GRAMMARIANS
Author: A. C. BURNELL

ON

THE AINDRA SCHOOL OF SANSKRIT GRAMMARIANS

THEIR PLACE IN THE SANSKRIT AND SUBORDINATE LITERATURES

BY

A. C. BURNELL, Ph. D.

Saktum iva tita-unā punanto yatra dhīrā manasā vācam akrata |
atra.....bhadrai 'shām laxmīr nihitā 'dhi vāci || Ṛ. V. x., 71, 2.

MANGALORE
BASEL MISSION BOOK & TRACT DEPOSITORY
LONDON 1875 BASEL
Trübner & Co. Missions-Buchhandlung

AN enquiry into the beginnings and history of Sanskrit Grammar is in itself an interesting subject, and has always been considered of importance since Profr. von Roth first opened the way[1], but it is at present imperatively necessary for several reasons, that something should be attempted, even if success be doubtful, and this must be my excuse for the present attempt.

Perhaps few will now assent to the late Profr. Goldstücker's claim on behalf of the Vedic commentators that they did not content themselves with copying their predecessors, but that they endeavoured to show "that the interpretations which they give are consistent with the grammatical requirements of the language itself"[2]. But whatever may be the value of the commentators application of Sanskrit Grammar to the interpretation of texts, the oldest treatises on that subject are the only remaining monuments of an important stage in the development of the Sanskrit language[3]. It is thus indispensable to the history of Indian thought, that it should be determined as ac-

1) By his "Zur Literatur und Geschichte des Weda" published in 1846. Since then our knowledge of this subject has been advanced in many ways by Weber, Benfey, Max Müller, Whitney, Regnier, Goldstücker, Kielhorn, Eggeling and others whose works I have quoted on nearly every page, and without which I could not have attempted this enquiry. Equally am I indebted to Senart's Pischel's and D'Alwis's works on Pali and Prakrit Grammar.

2) "Pāṇini's Place" (sep. imp.), p. 243.

3) Benfey ("Einleitung in die Grammatik der Vedischen Sprache" p. 3) says: "Dürfen wir unbedenklich die, wenn auch ziemlich grell klingende, Antithese aussprechen, dass uns von den Indern....auf der einen Seite die wunderbarste Sprache ohne eine sich auf sie stützende Grammatik hinterlassen ist, auf der andern dagegen die wunderbarste Grammatik ohne die Sprache, auf welche sie gestützt ist."

curately as possible, what is the condition of these texts, and under what influences they have been altered, if it cannot be assumed that they have been preserved intact. It then remains to see what principles guided the authors in their work.

Without a preliminary determination of these points it appears to me hazardous to use this great branch of Sanskrit literature as a means to solve historical problems, or for philological purposes. I have here attempted a new way of considering the problem—by examining what were the system and technical terms used before Pāṇini wrote his great work. It is well known that he was not the first, though he was the greatest of Indian grammarians, and chance having led me to discover a treatise which is said to be of the Aindra School, I soon found that the differences between the schools of Sanskrit Grammar must depend rather on system than on matter, and applying the scanty information which the Tolkāppiyam gave me, to the Sanskrit texts, I found that a number of hitherto unplaced works must represent the system or systems current before Pāṇini, though they cannot be in an intact condition. It cannot be for a moment supposed that Pāṇini's numerous predecessors did not differ in details of system, as well as in details of doctrine, but I think that, for the reasons I have given in this monograph, they all constitute a class which may be termed the Aindra School, as they agree among themselves in a marked way and equally differ from Pāṇini, as regards their system.

The historical value of Sanskrit texts being yet undetermined, I have thought it necessary to enquire briefly into this question, and have given my reasons for trusting, so far, the texts of grammatical works. This should logically come first, but briefly as I have treated the matter, it fills several pages, so I have put it as Appendix A.

The question I have enquired into in the first part, also requires an historical solution; a beginning is attempted in Appendix B.

Such enquiries as these are not only more necessary now than before, but are also possible at last. If the recollection of 1875 be rendered mournful to philologists by the loss of Ewald, Corssen, Bleek and Ebel, this year has seen the completion of grand works such as have never been done before—Böhtlingk and Roth's Sanskrit Dictionary and its necessary complement—Childers' Pali Dictionary. With these books at hand, Indian philologists must, and can, entertain larger views, and exercise a more fruitful activity than they have, as yet, ventured to do.

Tanjore,
1st *November* 1875.

A. B.

Transliteration.

For Sanskrit, I have used the system that I have always followed, and which is very near that used for Pali by Fausböll.

For Tamil̤̤, I have used the following:

a, ā, i, ī, u, ū, ĕ, e (long), ŏ, o (long), ai, au.

k (ɣ), ṅ; š (j), ń; ṭ (ḍ), ṇ; t (ð), n; p (b), m; y, r, l, v, l̤̤, ḷ, ṟ, *n*.

CONTENTS.

IV.

APPENDIX A.

APPENDIX B.

ON THE AINDRA GRAMMAR.

MUCH attention has been paid to the Sanskrit Grammars of late years, as perhaps the most remarkable part of the Indian literature excluding the Vedas[1]; but, as yet, little has been done to investigate the relations of the several acknowledged schools of grammarians, or to show their historical connexion.

Eight different schools of Grammar are commonly mentioned in India[2]. Of these, Pāṇini's system has long superseded all others; Çākaṭāyana's and Jinendra's are still known by existing MSS.; Candra (-gomin)'s Grammar exists in a Tibetan version[3], and four other schools (of Indra, Kāçakṛitsna, Āpiçali and Amara) are known by name or by an occasional quotation. Students of Sanskrit literature must have long ago remarked that this enumeration is apparently defective, as there is a large amount of grammatical literature (*e.g.* the Prātiçākhyas), existing in that language which cannot apparently be brought under any one of these schools, and must, thus, have been led to question the value of Vopadeva's statement; but I hope to be able to show here that this is not to be done. Of all the eight

---

1) Because (as far as we know) it is independent. *v.* Max Müller's "Ancient Sanskrit Literature" pp. 158, ffg. Aufrecht's "Uṇādi Sūtras" p. viii.

2) By Vopadeva (13th century), "Dhātupāṭha" (Introd. çl. 2.)

Indraç Candraḥ Kāçakṛitsn-'Āpiçalī Çakaṭāyanaḥ |
Pāṇiny-Amara-Jainendrā jayanty ashṭā 'diçābdikāḥ ||

This was first noticed by Colebrooke ("Essays", orig. ed. ii., p. 39). Vopadeva's date (12th century) is well known. (Aufrecht, "Catalogus" p. 174 *b.* etc.) Westergaard ("Radices Linguæ Sanskritæ" p. v.) puts him a little earlier but in the same century. He is said to have lived at Devagiri in the Deccan.

Durgācārya, in his commentary on Yāska (i., 20), says: "Vyākaraṇam ashṭadhā". I am unable to fix his date, but his style is modern.

3) To be found in the "Tandjur" (Bstan-hgyur); see Schiefner's article "Ueber die logischen und grammatischen Werke im Tandjur" (in "Bulletin de la classe des sciences historiques etca de l' Académie Impériale des sciences de Saint-Pétersbourg". iv. col. 294). No. 3604. "Candravyākaraṇasūtranāma. Luṅ-du ston-pa čandra-pa'i mdo śes-bya-va, in 6 capiteln." This was in sūtras as quotations by Xīrasvāmin and others show. It is said to approach Pāṇini's school. I should remark that the better known Grammar by Hemacandra (12th century) appears to be quoted occasionally as the Candra Grammar.

schools of Grammar already mentioned, that of Indra is the one which apparently is most open to doubt; the older grammarians (I believe) never mention the Aindra Grammar, and hence, the frequent references to it in other works seem questionable. I shall here give reasons for believing that the Aindra was the oldest school of the Sanskrit Grammarians; that Aindra treatises were actually known to, and quoted by Pāṇini and others; and that Aindra treatises still exist in the Prātiçākhyas, Kātantra and similar works, though they have been partly recast and corrected.

Firstly, I shall collect such references to the Aindra Grammar as I have been able to find, from the more recent up to the older Sanskrit literature, and in Chinese and Tibetan texts.

I.

In the twelfth century, besides the passage of Vopadeva, already quoted, we have a legend in the Kathāsaritsāgara of Somadeva of Cashmere. In this collection of stories, Kātyāyana the grammarian relates[1] that Varsha had a great many pupils among whom was Pāṇini, who was a sad dunce, and lazy in the service due to his teacher and his wife. Varsha's wife accordingly dismissed him, but he (the story runs) "grieved and desirous of knowledge went for penance to the Himalaya." There, "a new Grammar introductory to all science" was obtained by him from Induçekhara (Çiva) pleased by his stern austerity. "Having returned from thence, he challenged me (*i. e.* Kātyāyana) to a dispute, and seven days passed since the disputation of us two began. On the eighth day, he being conquered by me, at once a fearful noise was made by Çambhu in the sky. Thus my Aindra Grammar was destroyed on the

1) Ed. Brockhaus, i., p. 31 (Tar. iv., 20-25). This passage has already been quoted by Goldstücker and others.

Atha kālena Varshasya çishyavargo mahān abhūt |
tatrai 'ka*h* Pāṇinir nāma jaḍabuddhitaro 'bhavat ||
sa çuçrūshāpariklishṭa*h* preshito Varshabhāryayā |
agacchat tapase khinno vidyākāmo Himālayam ||
tatra tīvreṇa tapasā toshitād Induçekharāt |
sarvavidyāmukha*m* tena prāpta*m* vyākaraṇa*m* navam ||
tataç cā 'gatya mām eva vādāyā 'hvayate sma sa*h* |
pravṛitte cā 'vayor vāde prayātāh sapta vāsarā*h* ||
ashṭame 'hni mayā tasmin jite tatsamanantaram |
nabha*h*sthena mahāghoro hū*m*kāra*h* Çambhunā kṛita*h* ||
tena pranashṭam Aindra*m* tad asmadvyākaraṇa*m* bhuvi |
jitā*h* Pāṇinnā sarve mūrkhībhūtā vaya*m* puna*h* ||

earth; we all conquered by Pāṇini became stupid again." The story is an absurd one, and is useful only to show that an Aindra school of grammar was known in the 10th century and that it was said to have been superseded by Pāṇini's. It can, however, be traced back to a far older work, the "Bṛihatkathāmañjarī" (from which the "Kathāsaritsāgara" was compiled) of which I discovered some MSS. at Tanjore in 1871, and Dr. Bühler another (in 1872) in Gujarat[1]. Every feature of the story, as already told, is to be found here[2]. The date of the Bṛihatkathāmañjarī is uncertain, but it must be some centuries older than the Kathāsaritsāgara which belongs to the beginning of the twelfth century A. D.[3]

Hiouen-Thsang, the Chinese Buddhist pilgrim, who travelled in India from 629-645 A. D., mentions the town of Çālātura as being distinguished as Pāṇini's native place, and relates a story not quite unlike what has just been given. He says: "Dans la haute antiquité, les mots de la langue étaient extrêmement nombreux; mais quand le monde eut été détruit, l'univers se trouva vide et désert. Des dieux d'une longévité extraordinaire descendirent sur la terre pour servir de guides aux peuples. Telle fut l'origine des lettres et des livres. A partir de cette époque, leur source s'agrandit et dépassa les bornes. Le dieu Fan (Brahmā) et le roi du ciel (Indra) établirent des règles et se conformèrent au temps. Des Richis hérétiques composèrent chacun des mots. Les hommes les prirent pour modèles, continuèrent leur œuvre, et travaillèrent à l'envi pour en conserver la tradition; mais les étudiants faisaient de vains efforts, et il leur était difficile d'en approfondir le sens. A l'époque ou la vie des hommes était réduite à cent ans, on vit paraître le Richi Po-ni-ni (Pāṇini), qui était instruit dès sa naissance et possédait un vaste savoir. Affligé de l'ignorance du siècle, il voulut retrancher les notions vagues et fausses, débarasser la langue des mots superflus et en fixer les lois. Comme il voyageait pour faire des recherches et s'instruire, il rencontra le dieu Tseu-thsaï (Īçvara Dêva), et lui exposa

1) "*Academy*" for 15th Sept. 1871, p. 447. *Indian Antiquary* i., p. 302 ffg.

2) The text runs (Tanjore, 4880; Upakoçācaritam, çl. 8 ffg.):

Vyālendradattasahite sarvajñe mayi viçrute |
Pāṇinir nāma Varshasya çishyaḥ sarvajaḍāçrayaḥ ||
tapasā Çaṁkarāt prāpya navam vyākaraṇam vaçī |
dināny ashṭau vivāde me 'prativādisamo 'bhavat ||
mayā jite tatas tasmin hūṁkāreṇa vimohayan |
jahāra * * * * pād ai(n)dravyākaraṇasmṛitim || (°ṇaismṛi° MS. a reading which shows that this is a S. Indian MS.). No. 10.281 has the missing syllables supplied by a second hand—no Haraḥ ko(pād).

3) "Kathāsaritsāgara" Ed. Brockhaus, i., p. viii.

le plan de l'ouvrage qu'il méditait. "A merveille! lui dit le dieu Tseu-thsai; 'vous pouvez compter sur mon secours'. Après avoir reçu ses instructions, le Rĭchi se retira. Il se livra alors à des recherches profondes, et déploya toute la vigueur de son esprit. Il recueillit une multitude d'expressions, et composa un livre de mots[1] qui renfermait mille çlōkas; . . . . cet ouvrage est encore . . . . en grand honneur"[2].

Again in the life of Hiouen-Thsang (by his contemporaries Hoeï-Li and Yen-Thsong) in the account of the learned monk's study of Sanskrit at the convent of Nālanda, we find the following: "Il étudia à la fois les livres des Brāhmanes et l'ouvrage appelé Ki-lun, qui traite des caractères Fan de l' Inde. Leur origine se perd dans l'antiquité, et personne ne sait qui les a inventés. Au commencement des Kalpas, le roi Fan (Brahmā) les expliqua le premier, et les transmit aux Dēvas et aux hommes. Comme ces caractères furent expliqués par Brahmâ, on les appela pour cette raison Fan-chou ou Écriture de Brahmā. Le texte primitif était fort étendu et embrassait un million de çlôkas. C'est l'ouvrage qu'on appelait anciennement Pi-kia-lo-lun; mais cette prononciation est incorrecte. Pour être exact, il faut dire Pi-ye-kie-la-nan (Vyâkaraṇam), mot que l'on traduit par Ching-ming-ki-lun (Traité mnémonique pour la connaissance des sons). On lui a donné ce nom, parcequ'il renferme, d'une manière fort étendue, toutes les règles de la langue, et sert à les expliquer avec clarté. Dans l'antiquité, au commencement du Kalpa parfait (Siddhakalpa?), le roi Fan (Brahmā) fut le premier à l' expliquer; il comprenait alors un million de çlôkas. Ensuite, au commencement du Kalpa stationnaire (Sthitakalpa?), Ti-chi (Indra) l'abrégea et le rédigea en cent mille çlokas. Enfin, dans le royaume de Gandhara, de l'Inde du Nord, un brâhmane nommé le Rĭchi Po-ni-ni (Pâṇini), de la ville de Tou-lo (Çālātura), l'abrégea encore et le rédigea en huit mille çlōkas. C'est l'ouvrage qui est maintenant en usage dans l'Inde. Dans ces derniers temps, un brāhmane l'abrégea encore, à la demande d'un roi de l'Inde du Sud où il était né, et le rédigea en deux mille cinq cents çlōkas. Cette édition est fort répandue dans les royaumes des frontières; mais les savants de l'Inde ne la suivent point."[3]

---

1) Profr. Max Müller has identified this (in Chinese Tseu-chou, "un livre de charactères") with "Çabdānuçāsanam" the real title of Pāṇini's work. (A. S. Lit. p. 306, n.)

2) "Mémoires sur les Contrées Occidentales" by St. Julien i., pp. 125-7.

3) "Histoire de la vie de Hiouen-Thsang" by St. Julien pp. 165-6.

A brief summary of the grammatical system of Pāṇini follows, which is so correct as to show conclusively that the previous passage (given above) may be taken as a fair statement of the Indian notions regarding the origin of the science of grammar as they passed current in the 7th century A. D.

Again the Buddhist canonical works of the North mention the Indra Grammar; in the Avadānaçataka it is stated that Çāriputra learned it as a boy.[1)]

In the literature of Tibet, which consists almost exclusively of servile translations of the Sanskrit canonical books known to the Buddhists of N. India in the seventh and following centuries and of compilations from that source, the Indra Grammar is mentioned more than once. Bu-ston states that the first grammar was composed by Sarvajñāna (*i. e.* Çiva), but this never came to Jambudvīpa. Then Indra compiled the Indravyākaraṇa which Bṛihaspati studied. This was current in Jambudvīpa, but was surpassed by Pāṇini's work[2)].

Tāranātha (a Tibetan Lama) compiled in 1608 A. D. a very remarkable history of Buddhism in India, in which he, more than once, alludes to the Indra Grammar, and though the information he gives is clearly secondary, it substantially agrees with what the Sanskrit authors tell us. In his account of Pāṇini (whom he makes out to have lived under Nanda or in the fourth century B. C.), he states that though it is said in Tibet that the Indravyākaraṇa is earlier, this must be held of the region of the gods, and not of Āryadeça. He adds that Pandits say that the Candravyākaraṇa agrees with Pāṇini's, and the Kalāpa with the Indra Grammar[3)].

Again in another place, Tāraṇātha, after relating a legend about the snake-king Çesha's explanation of Pāṇini's work (a legend I have often heard in S. India), goes on to relate that a Brahman named Saptavarman[4)] asked Shaṇmukha (or Kārttikeya) to reveal to him the Indra Grammar, on which the god began: "Siddho varṇasamāmnāyaḥ," and Saptavarman

---

1) Burnouf "Introduction" i., p. 456 "à seize ans il avait lu la grammaire d' Indra et vaincu tous ceux qui disputaient avec lui." cfr. Lassen's I. A—K. ii., (2nd ed.) p. 477. On the period of this rather late (secondary or Mahāyāna) work see Wassiljew's "Der Buddhismus" p. 332.

2) Wassiljew in Schiefner's translation of Tāranātha's Tibetan History of Indian Buddhism, p. 294.

3) Tāranātha's History of Indian Buddhism, p. 43 (Tibetan text) and p. 54 (of Schiefner's German translation).

4) The Sanskrit MSS. appear to have Sarvavarman, but Tāranātha expressly states that this is wrong, as also Īçvaravarman.

thereon at once comprehended all the rest. This Sūtra is actually the first of the Kātantra (or Kalāpa grammar), and this grammar is certainly of the Aindra school. Tāranātha makes Saptavarman a contemporary of Kālidāsa and Nāgārjuna[1]. In another place a Brahman named Indradhruva is said to have had this grammar revealed to him, and that it contained 25,000 çlokas[2].

The miraculous part of all these legends may be fairly put down to the theological nature of the civilization prevailing at the times the several authors wrote or compiled their books. That Tāranātha had really historical records at his disposal is shown by Profr. Wassiljew in the preface to his Russian translation of Tāranātha[3].

When we get to the centuries before our era, with one remarkable exception, all mention of the Indra Grammar appears to be wanting. In the third section of this paper, I shall show that Pāṇini really quotes this grammar (or rather school of grammarians) under the name of the prāñca*h* (teachers); but the only direct mention of the Indra Grammar in the old Sanskrit literature that I can find, is in a quotation by Sāyaṇa from a Brāhmaṇa as yet not identified. This mentions Indra as the original grammarian[4].

So much for references which can be shown to be trustworthy, and to belong to tolerably certain periods of Indian history. There are other allusions but of uncertain date and value; such as: "Aindri vāg iva" in the Bhojacampū (of the 16th century), and "Yathārtha*m* padam Aindrāṇām" in Durgācārya's Niruktavṛitti.

The commentary on the Sārasvatavyākaraṇa also mentions Indra as the first grammarian[5].

> "Indrādayo 'pi yasyā 'nta*m* na yayu*h* çabdavāridhe*h* |
> prakriyāntasya kṛitsnasya xamo vaktu*m* nara*h* katham" ||

---

1) *u. s.* pp. 60 and 75 respectively.

2) *u. s.* pp. 58 and 66. Wassiljew's "Der Buddhismus," p. 58, *n*.

3) Also translated separately into German by Schiefner. It is necessary to remark that the Tibetan has Tāranātha, and not Tārānātha as one would expect.

4) It occurs in Sāyaṇa's introduction to his commentary on the Ṛig-Veda (vol. i., p. 35, ed. Max Müller) and runs: "Vāg vai parācy avyākṛitā 'vadat te devā indram abruvann imā*m* no vāca*m* vyākurv iti | so 'bravīd vara*m* vṛiṇai mahya*m* cai 'vai 'sha vāyave ca saha gṛihyātā iti tasmād aindravāyava*h* saha pragṛihyate | tām indro madhyato 'vakramya vyākarot | tāsmād iyam vyākṛitā vāg udyata iti." | Sāyaṇa understands this to refer to grammatical analysis of words, which is the obvious meaning.

5) Bombay edition, çloka 2.

These references are to the old original Aindra Grammar, but there are others which appear to refer to a modern Indra or Jaine-'ndra (as he appears to have been called to distinguish him from the god Indra the supposed author of the Aindra Grammar), who lived some time before the 12th century A. D. Vopadeva, it should be remarked, places him the last of the eight grammarians he mentions[1].

Thus, the references in Jain books to a grammarian named Indra appear to refer to this grammar. For example, the actual grammatical text-book of the Jains which passes under the name of Çākaṭāyana, quotes the opinion of an Indra; the commentary (by Yaxavarman) explains this name by Indra Ācārya, and this is the author of the Jainendra Grammar, in all probability, as he teaches what is directed by this rule[2].

The age and authenticity of this Çākaṭāyanavyākaraṇa are as yet undetermined. Profr. Bühler[3] considers it to be the real work that Pāṇini quotes; but the late Profr. Goldstücker was always in doubt about it[4]. If I may express an opinion, it is (as I hope to show) a comparatively modern recast of an old work. Yaxavarman the commentator on the Çākaṭāyana Grammar also mentions an Indra in his preface: "Indracandrādibhiḥ çābdair yad uktam çabdalaxaṇam"; but the age of this author is not known, and this çloka is evidently a copy of Vopadeva's statement.

To multiply these allusions (as I believe could be done), would be of no use; for the decisive passages I have quoted, which are from books of widely different times and sects, Brahmanical and Buddhist, and from different parts of India, show that there once existed a Sanskrit Grammar known as the Indra Grammar, and that it was said to have been superseded by the work of Pāṇini; also that it was reputed to have been the earliest Sanskrit Grammar. Indian legends are historically worthless,

---

1) This Jinendra is perhaps quoted by Ujjvaladatta in his Commentary on the Uṇādi Sūtras (Pāṇinīya). He must have lived about 1250 A. D. See Aufrecht's edition, p. xiv.

2) i. 2, 37 "Jarāyā ṅas Indrasyā 'ci". C. Jarāçabdasya tatsambandhiny anyasambandhini vā ajādau supi pare Indrasyā 'cāryasya matena ṅasādeço bhavati | jarasau jarasaḥ | etc." The Jainendra Grammar (p. 21 of Madras MS. 1461) has jarāyā ṅas. This passage has been kindly found for me by my friend Profr. Oppert. That the Çākaṭāyana Grammar quotes Āryavajra and Indra (and these only as far as I have seen) was first pointed out by Dr. Bühler, but without mentioning the place ("Orient und Occident", iii. p. 182). Is this Jinendra the author of the "Nyāsa" a pañjikā on the Kāçikāvṛitti which is also cited by Vopadeva? (Colebrooke's "Essays" ii., p. 40.)

3) "Orient und Occident" ii., pp. 691 ffg.

4) "Pāṇini's Place" p. 153 *n*. The doubts he expressed hesitatingly here, he stated much more fully in conversations with me in 1869 and 1870.

but the passages I have quoted show that at several distant parts of India, and at remote dates such a book did exist, and that Vopadeva did not retail some idle fiction in mentioning an Aindra School of Grammar. This fact having been ascertained, it is now possible to follow up the clues which I have found to the determination of the works belonging to this school, and to trace their general characteristics.

II.

The fact that an Indra Grammar was commonly reported in India and elsewhere to have preceded that by Pāṇini, early attracted my attention[1], and for several years I had diligent search made for this important work in all parts of S. India. It is needless to say that I had MSS. described to me with great detail, and more than once; but not even a line was ever produced, and after some years waiting, I almost made up my mind that the Aindra Grammar was one of the fictions so common in India, and gave up the search. I then turned to the grammars of the so-called Dravidian languages, which, as they are often of considerable age and imitations of Sanskrit works would, I hoped, throw some light on the schools of Sanskrit grammar; I soon found that the Tamiḻ and Canarese grammars had the same technical terms as the Prātiçākhyas, Kātantra, and some others; and as it is the oldest Tamiḻ grammar and, therefore, the oldest of the kind in S. India, I turned to the Tolkāppiyam, as it seemed likely to furnish the best information. Like all classical Tamiḻ works, this grammar has a preface by a contemporary of the author, in this case one Pa*n*ambara*n*, who certifies (as I found to my surprise) that the "ainðira-niṟainða-tolkāppiyam", *i.e.* "Tolkāppiyam full of (or according to) the Aindra (system)" was read in Pāṇḍiya*n*'s (*i.e.* the Madura king's) assembly, and approved by Aðaṅkōṭṭāšā*n*[2]. The author, Tolkāppiyan, was a Buddhist or Jain, and is unquestionably one of the oldest Tamiḻ authors. The earliest commentator on this grammar, Našši*n*ārkki*n*iyar, was also originally a Buddhist, but became a convert to the Çaiva doctrine. It is thus impossible to put the original text much later than the eighth century; for by the tenth century the whole Pāṇḍiya kingdom

---

1) I first found this fact stated in Profr. Weber's "Indische Literaturgeschichte" p. 167 *n*.

2) "Tolkāppiyam", edited by Maγāliṅγaiyar, (Madras, çāl. ç. 1770 4°.) p. 1. My discovery of this clue was announced in the *Academy* early in 1874. (Vol. V.)

had fallen under the orthodox Colas. There is nothing to throw doubt on these statements which could have been made for no possible reason if untrue. This discovery at once clears up a difficulty in the Indian accounts of the Sanskrit Schools of Grammar by bringing the hitherto unclassified works (which I have already mentioned) into their place. It also enables one to trace out the chief characteristics of this Aindra School. To do this, I shall now compare the arrangement and technical words of the Tolkāppiyam with those of the Kātantra, Kaccāyana's Pāli Grammar[1], and the Prātiçākhyas. I shall first show that the general arrangement of all is much the same. This may be termed the natural arrangement as opposed to the artificial arrangement of Pāṇini. In the latest grammars which re-arrange Pāṇini's matter in much the same way[2], we see, probably, a reversion to the simpler and older system. The first two sections[3] of the Tolkāppiyam only are of interest here, and owing to the limited scope of the Prātiçākhyas[4] it is only possible to compare some of the technical terms used in them with those of the other more extensive grammars. I shall occasionally refer to the Na*nn*ūl also. This is the most commonly used Tamiḻ grammar, and is a professed recast and expansion, in some respects, of the Tolkāppiyam, but with more Sanskrit terms and close reference to the Kātantra. The date of its composition is apparently some centuries after the Tolkāppiyam, and also after the fall of the great Tamiḻ kingdoms in the 14th century A. D.

That the arrangement of the Kātantra, Kaccāyana's Pāli Grammar, and the Tolkāppiyam is really the same will be seen by the following comparative table:

---

1) The close connection between Kaccāyana's Pāli Grammar and the Kātantra was noticed first by J. d'Alwis and E. Kuhn ("Kaccāyanappakaraṅae Specimen", pp. 19-21). cfr. Senart's edition of the Pāli Grammar, p. 2, and Weber's "Indische Streifen" ii., p. 324. I do not find that any one noticed the connection between the Kātantra and the Prātiçākhyas etc.

2) The Prakriyākaumudī and Siddhāntakaumudī.

3) The whole comprises three sections: the first contains phonetics and sandhi; the second forms and syntax; the third comprises rhetoric and prosody.

4) Cfr. Goldstücker (in the "*Academy*" vol. i., p. 270): "The Prātiçākhyas, therefore, are not grammars; for grammars have to deal with the etymon of words and with the whole range of linguistic facts, but they are *grammatical works*, in the sense in which this term is commonly applied to works dealing with grammatical subjects in general, or some grammatical topic in particular, for they must teach the phonetic changes which padas undergo." See also Prof. Whitney's remarks (Ath. pr. p. 249).

Tolkāppiyam	Kātantra	Kaccāyana
A. Eḻuttaðiγāram (*Letters*)	Sandhi-prakaraṇa	Sandhi-kappa
§1. Description of Alphabet, enumeration of letters, and classes of letters.	§1. Description of Alphabet, enumeration of letters, and classes of letters.	§1. Description of Alphabet, enumeration of letters, and classes of letters.
2. Peculiar letters.	2. Sandhi of vowels.	2. Sandhi of vowels.
3. Pronunciation.	3. Exceptions.	3. Exceptions.
4. Sandhi.	4. Sandhi of consonants.	4. Sandhi of niggahītam[1].
5. Do.	5. Do. *h* etc.	5. Sandhi of prepositions.
6. Sandhi of case terminations in nouns.		
7. Sandhi of final vowels.		
8. Do. consonants.		
9. Do. shortened u.		
B. ii. Sŏllaðiγāram (*Words*)	Nāmacatushṭaya etc.	Nāma-kappa etc.
1. General.	1. Technical terms for cases; terminations; inflection.	1. Case terminations and inflection of nouns.
2. Cases and their meanings.	2. Do.	2. Pronouns etc.
3. Substitution of cases.	3. Pronouns.	3. Irregular nouns.
4. Vocative case.	4. Kāraka.	4.
5. Of nouns (pĕyarššŏl).	5. Samāsa.	5. Substitutes for cases, degrees of comparison.
	6. Taddhita.	6. Kāraka.
		7. Samāsa.
		8. Taddhita.
C.	Ākhyātaprakaraṇa	Ākhyāta-kappa
6. Verbs (vinaiššŏl).	1. Voices; tenses etc.	1. Voices; tenses; person endings.
	2. Classes of verbs etc.	2. Classes of verbs.
	3. Reduplication etc.	3. Reduplication; irregular verbs.
	4. Samprasāraṇa.	
	5. Guṇa.	
	6. Anushaṅga.	4.
	7. Idāgama.	
	8.	
	Kṛit-affixes	Kita-kappa
There are no such formations in Tamiḻ.	1.	1. Kṛit-affixes.
	2.	2.
	3.	3.
	4.	4.
D.	5.	5.
7. On particles (iḍaiššŏl)	6. Alam, khalu etc.	
E.		
8. Peculiar words (uriššŏl)		
9. Construction etc.		

1) "Grammaire Palie" (Minayeff) p. 49. "bindu niggahītam"; "Kaccāyana" (by Senart), p. 10.

It is obvious that the arrangement of all these grammars is simple and natural. First (A) come phonetics and an elaborate description of the alphabet, a feature of the Prātiçākhyas also. Next come the four parts of speech treated in order (B. C. D. E.) and in a simple manner compared with the elaborate and intricate plan of Pāṇini. The identity of the plans of the Kātantra and Kaccāyana needs no illustration; the Tolkāppiyam varies (as regards E.) owing to the impossibility of arranging the Tamiḻ elements in exactly the same way as the Sanskrit, Prakrit or Pāli, and as the uriššōl words constitute an artificial class.

The arrangement of the Pāṇinīya Grammar in eight books is as follows:

I. Technical terms; special use of the numbers; ekaçesha; rules of interpretation of the sūtras; use of the Ātmanepada and Parasmaipada; explanation of technical terms.

II. Samāsa; use of cases; affixes.

III., IV., V. Affixes which form verbs and nouns.

VI., VII. Augment and reduplication; accent; inflection.

VIII. Special rules; rules of euphony[1].

The Grammars which now bear the names of Çākaṭāyana and Jinendra[2], though in fewer chapters, follow the same highly artificial plan which is intended to economise space, and reduce the sūtras to the narrowest possible limits.

Thus the Aindra Grammars are on a simpler and more natural plan which is understood at first sight, while Pāṇini's Grammar is, except to the initiated, in hopeless confusion[3].

If the arrangements of the matter in the Aindra and Pāṇinīya Grammars differ widely, still more so do the technical terms. In the former these are ordinary words for the most part, though used with a somewhat special meaning. In the latter they are nearly all highly artificial abbreviations or letters used with a particular conventional value assigned

1) For a more detailed account see Böhtlingk's edition of Pāṇini, vol. ii., pp. xxiv-xxxvi.

2) Dr. Bühler has already pointed out the existence of these two grammars in "Orient und Occident", vol. ii., p. 182. The Jinendra Grammar is among the Leyden MSS. at Madras, and is a Jain MS. Of Çākaṭāyana there are fragments in the same collection, and a complete copy of the text and Uṇādisūtras (in the Malayāḷam character) among the MSS. I presented to the India Office Library in 1870. I have since procured other complete MSS. of the text, commentary etc., which I have used here. All these are Jain MSS. from the Canarese country.

3) See Colebrooke's remarks, "Essays", ii., pp. 5-8. Note especially P. viii., 2, 1.

to them; they are not, in short, really words. The agreement between the technical terms of the Tolkāppiyam on the one hand and Kātantra and similar works on the other is close, while they have really little in common with those of Pāṇini, though some of their terms are to be found in the latter. The Grammars which I thus class together have certain marked differences with one another in respect of a very few technical terms. These are important as marking stages of development, but I shall reserve discussion of them till I come to that subject, and meanwhile remark on the coincidences only.

The first point to be remarked is the fourfold division of words (pada) into: nāman (noun), ākhyāta (verb), upasarga (preposition), and nipāta (particle). This division is found in Yāska[1], and the terms occur in the Kātantra[2], Kaccāyana[3], and the Prātiçākhyas[4]. In Tamiḻ the four classes of words are called pĕyarššŏl, vinaiššŏl, iḍaiššŏl, and uriššŏl[5]; literally: name-word, act-word, middle-word, peculiar-word. The first is a literal translation of the Sanskrit nāma(-pada), the second is for kriyā; ākhyāta being, apparently, untranslatable in Tamiḻ. The two last differ from the Aindra terms, but for the reason that the Tamiḻ language has nothing corresponding to the prepositions and particles of Sanskrit. Iḍaiššŏl means middle-word, and is the name of affixes and the letters inserted between the root and suffix to express the tense; uriššŏl 'peculiar-

---

1) ed. Roth. p. 31 (Nir. i., 1). Profr. Weber ("In. Studien" iv., p. 76) has already remarked the general identity of the technical terms used by Yāska and the Kātyāyanīya Prātiçākhya (of the White Yajur Veda).

2) Nāmacatushṭaya and ākhyātaprakaraṇa are the names of the sections on nouns and verbs. Nāma also occurs in ii., 5, 1 etc. The last chapter is on particles. Nipāta occurs in i., 3, 1.

3) Nāma, iv., 1. Akhyātakappa is the title of the sixth section of the work. Upasarga—i., 5, 10, and in the same place Nipāta also.

4) 1. Ṛig.V. Pr. xii., 5-8. Nāmākhyātam upasargo nipātaç catvāry āhu*h* padajātāni çabdā*h* etc. I quote this from Regnier's edition, as unfortunately, I have not got Profr. Max Müller's at hand. It must be remarked that the chapter in which this text occurs seems to be an addition to the original text.

2. Taitt. Prātiç (ed. Whitney) i., 15; vi., 4; x., 9; xiv., 8 (u p a s a r g a). But few technical terms of general grammar occur in this work. See Profr. Whitney's remarks on p. 432.

3. Atharva Prātiç (ed. Whitney) i., 1. "caturṇā*m* padajātānā*m* nāmākhyātopasarga-nipātānā*m* sandhyapadyau guṇau prātijñam".

4. Kātyāyanīya Prātiçākhya of the White Yajur Veda (ed. Weber, in "In. Studien" iv.) *a* viii., 52. "Tac(padam) caturdhā nāmākhyātopasarganipātā*h*" etc. This is, however, from a chapter which is probably not part of the original work. Nipāta occurs in ii., 16.

5) For these terms see chapters 5-8 of Tolk. ii. which treat of the four kinds of words in the order given above. cfr. Nan*n*ūl (Pĕyariyal) i., 18.

word' is the name of adjectives and adverbs. In Tamiḻ there are no prepositions or prefixes. Pada[1] occurs in all these works as the term for a word.

Now in Pāṇini the parts of speech are treated in a more complicated way, and only upsarga and nipāta are there found, though not with quite the same significations as in the Aindra Grammar[2].

For nāma we find sup and subanta, and for ākhyāta we find tiṅ[3]; both artificial technical terms, and belonging to a far more advanced stage of analysis. It is sufficient to point out here that for the old simple terms, we find in Pāṇini an elaborate classification of nouns and verbs to suit the grammatical forms and irregularities; the analysis is no longer philosophical, but according to the forms.

The Tamiḻ Grammar supplies another division of words which we do not find in the Sanskrit and Pāli Grammars, viz: into paɣupaδam and paɣāpaδam, literally: divisible and indivisible words. These words are nothing more than partial translations of the terms iṅgyapada and aniṅgyapada which occur in all the Prātiçākhyas. The commentary of Uvaṭa on the Ṛigvedaprātiçākhya (i., çl. 25) explains the word iṅgya: "iṅgyaçabdena sāvagraham padam ucyate". Avagraha is a pause which divides the component parts of a compound[4].

As regards the terms relating to phonetics, the identity is nearly complete. In the Tolkāppiyam a vowel is called uyir[5], that is, 'breath'

---

1) Kāt. ii., 5, 5; Kacc. iv., 8; Ṛik. pr. ii., 12; Taitt. pr. i., 54; Atharva pr. iii., 95; Kātyāyanīya pr. i., 98. Pratijñāsūtra, 9. In the Tolkāppiyam, mŏḻi (=word), being a translation of pada, is alone used, it appears. In the *Nannūl*, paδa is preferred (ii., 1, 1); šŏl with the sense of word is also used.

2) Goldstücker ("Pāṇini's Place" pp. 224-5) has well shown the development in Pāṇini's view of nipātas. He says: "Pāṇini teaches that the first and general category to which prepositions belong, is that of n i p ā t a s or particles: he then continues, that they are u p s a r g a s when they are joined to "verbal action" (*i. e.* to a verb); g a t i s, if the verbal root to which they are attached become developed into a noun; and that they are k a r m a p r a v a c a n ī y a s if they are detached and govern a noun. Of such a distinction there is no trace in the Nirukta". On p. 222 Goldstücker shows that Pāṇini used the term upsarga without definition, and that, consequently, it was already in use. Yāska, however, defines it.

3) Or in the usual practice tiṅanta. The Chinese form of this word has been strangely misunderstood by St. Julien ("Histoire de la vie de Hiouen-Thsang", pp. 166 and 167), who puts tryanta (!) for the ti-yen-to of the Chinese text.

4) Regnier says: "mobile, séparable; c'est à dire, divisé en deux parties dans le p a d a."

Paɣu (in Tamiḻ) is to divide or separate; paɣā is the negative form. These terms appear first in the *Nannūl*. The Aniṅgyalaxaṅa has: aniṅgyam iti bhāgapadam na tv asamāsapadam.

5) Tolk. i., 1, 8.

or 'life'. In the Kātantra[1], in the Prātiçākhyas[2] and Kaccāyana[3], svara or sara (in Pāli) is used for 'vowel'. This word is obviously the original of 'uyir'; svara means sound and breath also. A consonant in the Tolkāppiyam[4] is 'mĕy', 'feeling' (the sense) or 'body'; that is an evident translation of the Sanskrit sparça which is a name of the consonants k to m[5]. The Kātantra and Kaccāyana use only the *general* term for all the consonants[6]—vyañjana—which appears in the Prātiçākhyas with the same sense[7]. European students of the Tamiḻ grammar without exception appear to have been ignorant that it is a mere adaptation from the Sanskrit, and have invented a pretty little allegory about consonants being the body and vowels the life, which thus falls to the ground: for the terms used, in reality, refer to the physiological nature of the sounds, and are scientific not fanciful. Vowels are 'short' (kuṟil = hrasva) and 'long' (neḍil = dīrgha)[8]. The Tamiḻ Grammar divides the consonants into vali 'strong', meli 'soft', and iḍai or 'medial'[9]. The first (k, š, ṭ, t, p) and second (ṅ, ń, ṇ, n, m) do not correspond to the aghosha and ghoshavat classes of the Sanskrit and Pāli Grammars; the difference in name is owing to the peculiar phonetic system of Tamiḻ which differs altogether from the Sanskrit. The iḍai (or medial) letters (y, r, l, v, ḷ and ḻ) correspond with the Sanskrit anta*h*sthā*h*[10] and the Tamiḻ name is an exact translation of the Sanskrit. Letters are said in the Tamiḻ to belong to an iṇam or class (=varga)[11]. The Sanskrit works have a term for the sibilants (ūshmāna*h*) which is common to them[12], but the Tamiḻ and Pāli phonetic systems want corresponding classes. The term for the

1) Kāt. i., 1, 2, and 7 etc.

2) Ṛik. pr. i., 1. Taitt. pr. i., 5. Atharva pr. i., 4. Kātyāyanīya pr. i., 39, etc. Pāṇinīyaçīxā, çl. 4.

3) Kaccāyana, i., 1, 3.

4) Tolk. i., 1, 9.

5) Ṛik. pr. i. 2. Uvaṭa says: "teshā*m* vyañjanānām ādyā vargā*h* sparçasañjñā veditavyā*h* | spashṭakaraṇā*h* sparçā*h* kādayo māntā*h*." (Tanjore MS. 2,417.)

Taitt. pr. i., 7 etc. Atharva pr. i., 6. Kāty. pr. i., 49. Pāṇinīyaçīxā, çl. 4. Maṇḍūkaçīxā (quoted by Profr. Weber) 5, 8. and in similar works.

6) Kāt. i., 1, 9. Kacc. i., 1, 6.

7) Ṛik. pr. i., 1. Taitt. pr. i., 6. Atharva pr. i., 43. Kāt. pr. i., 38.

8) Tolk. i., 1, 3-4.

9) Do. i., 1, 19-21.

10) Kāt. i., 1. 14. Ṛik. pr. i., 2; Atharva pr. i., 30; Kāty. pr. iii., 129; Pratijñāsūtra 9, 17. Pāṇinīyaçīxā 7.

11) Tolk. ii., 1, 18; Kāt. i., 1, 10, etc.; Kacc. i., 1, 7; Ṛik. pr. i., 2; Taitt. pr. i., 10 etc.

12) Atharva pr. ii., 38. Kātyāyanīya pr. i., 64 etc. Pāṇinīyaçīxā, çl. 15. Pratijñāsūtra 9.

union of one letter with another is in all the Sanskrit works and in Kaccāyana also, sandhi; the same is preserved in the Tamil̤ sanδi.

As regards the names of letters the Tolkāppiyam affixes -aγaram[1] to consonants, -γaram[2] to short vowels and -γāram[3] to long. This is obviously an extended application of the use of -kāra which occurs in all the Sanskrit treatises including Pāṇini's[4].

There are also some terms relative to phonetics, which are common to the Kātantra and to some of the Prātiçākhyas, though they are absent from Kaccāyana's Grammar and the Tolkāppiyam; for Pāli and Tamil̤ present nothing to which they can be applied. Such is nāmin as a name of the vowels, except a, ā[5]; common to all (except Kaccāyana) is sandhyaxara[6] = combined letter or diphthong, but such a term would be superfluous in Pāli and Tamil̤ Grammars. Again samāna as a name of the vowels a to lṛī is common to the same[7].

Compared with this system, that of Pāṇini is at once seen to be totally different. In it there is no occasion for a classification of letters as described, for that is effected in a different way by the aid of the Çiva-sūtras. The use of varga to name a class of letters (*e.g.* ka-varga = k, kh, etc.) is replaced in Pāṇini's system by the single letter u suffixed; thus ku has the same meaning as kavarga. Thus, of the above words mentioned as occurring in the Aindra treatises, only two (hrasva and dīrgha[8]) occur in Pāṇini, and then as no part of his system, but merely explanatory.

Distinction is made as to the place in the vocal organs by which the letters are pronounced, and which is called iḍam[9] (place) the literal translation of sthāna which occurs in the Prātiçākhyas[10]. In the Na*nn*ūl iḍam and tānam (*i.e.* sthāna) are indiscriminately used[11]. Iḍam is fourfold— uṛam (breast), kaṇḍam (throat), uššì (head), and mūkku (nose)

---

1) Tolk. i., 1, 1.

2) Do. i., 1, 2.

3) Do. i, 1, 3.

4) See Goldstücker's "Pāṇini's Place" pp. 35-42. We find in the Na*nn*ūl a further development of this terminology, viz: -kāṇ as the name of the foreign ai and au (Na*nn*ūl ii., 43). That this is an innovation appears clearly from Tolk. i., 1, 3.

5) Kāt. i., 1, 7. Ṛik. pr. i, 17, etc. and Atharva pr. ii., 29.

6) Kāt., i., 1, 8. Ṛik. pr. i., 1. Atharva pr. i., 40. Kātyāyanīya pr. i., 45.

7) Kāt. i., 1, 8. Ṛik. pr. i., 1. Taitt. pr. i, 2. Atharva pr. iii., 42.

8) Pāṇini i., 2, 27.

9) Tolk. i., 3, 1.

10) Ṛik. pr. i., 10 and 11. Taitt. pr. ii., 31. Atharva pr. i., 41. Kātyāyanīya pr. i., 43.

11) Na*nn*ūl ii., 17 and 20.

which obviously correspond with the Sanskrit— uras, kaṇṭha, mūrddhan and nāsa[1]. The enumeration of these sthānas differs much in the Sanskrit phonetic treatises. With regard to the pronunciation of letters, muyaṟši[2] (exertion) is also distinguished; this is an exact translation of prayatna[3]. For sthāna Pāṇini has āsya, prayatna he retains[4].

The length of utterance of a letter is marked by one or more māttirai[5], which is the Tamiḻ form of the Sanskrit mātrā[6]. This term does not occur in Pāṇini.

Coming to the technical words relating to inflection, it is again evident that the Tamiḻ terms are nothing but translations of the Sanskrit. The term for case in the Tolkāppiyam is vēṟṟumai='distinguishing'[7]; this is the obvious translation of the Sanskrit vibhakti, which is common to all the works I have grouped together[8]. The cases in Tamiḻ are first, second etc.[9], answering to the Sanskrit prathamā, dvitīyā etc.[10], and the number and use of the cases is made to agree with that of the Sanskrit Grammar, though very unnecessarily. Thus seven cases and the vocative, or eight[11] are reckoned. In the Kātantra etc., the vocative is called āmantrita or āmantraṇa[12]; in Tamiḻ it is called viḷi[13] or 'calling' the exact translation of the former.

---

1) The Nāradaçīxā (i., 7) knows only three (uraḥ kaṇṭhaç çiraç cai'va sthānāni trīṇi vāṅ maye); the Kāty. pr. mentions three (i., 10); the Pāṇinīyaçīxā (13) has eight, like the Maṇḍūkīçīxā.

2) Cfr. Nannūl ii., 17.

3) Ṛik. pr. xiv., 10. Taitt. pr. xvii., 6. Pāṇinīyaçīxā, çl. 12.

4) Pāṇini, i., 1, 9.

5) Tolk. i., 1, 7. cfr. Nannūl, ii., 44-5. The Pāṇinīyaçīxā (v. 49) and Ṛik. pr. (xiii., 18) explains the length of sounds of one, two or three mātrās by the cries of certain animals. Here in the Tamiḻ books it is measured by the "winking of the eye" or "snapping the fingers".

6) Ṛikpr. i., 6. Atharva pr. i., 38; Kāty. pr. i., 54; Pāṇinīyaçīxā, çl. 16.

7) ii., 2, 1. Beschi ("Clavis" § p. 18) says: "Casus appellant veṟṟumai, quasi differentia nominis". So the Commentator Durgasimha says (on Kāt. ii., 1, 1, 2): "arthasya vibhañjanād vibhaktaya iti".

8) Kāt. ii., 1, 1; Kacc. ii., 1, 3; Atharva. pr. ii., 51; Kāty. pr. v, 13.

9) Tolk. ii, 2, 10 ffg.

10) 1. prathamā—Kāt. ii., 2, 17. Kacc. iii., 14.—2. dvitīyā—Kāt. ii., 1, 44; Kacc. iii., 27.—3. tritīyā—Kāt. ii., 1, 7; Kacc. iii., 16.—4. caturthī—Kāt. ii., 3, 1; Kacc. iii, 23.—5. pañcamī—Kāt. ii., 4, 20; Kacc. ii., 5, 2.—6. shashṭhī—Kāt. ii., 3, 1; Kacc. iii., 31.—7. saptamī—Kāt. ii., 4, 2; Kacc. ii., 5, 3. It is not worth while collecting the few references in the Prātiçākhyas etc.

11) Tolk. ii., 2, 2.

12) Kāt. ii, 1, 5; Ṛik. pr. i., 18; Atharva. pr. i, 81; Kāty. pr. ii., 17. Kacc. ii., 1, 5, has ālapana.

13) Tolk. ii., 2, 2.

Some of these terms occur in Pāṇini, but they form no real part of the system he uses; by it the names of cases are the case-terminations with indicative letters attached. For the name of the vocative, besides āmantrita we find in Pāṇini the term sambuddhi, which is equivalent to it, and which also occurs in the Kātantra.

The technical terms with regard to verbs also show much the same likeness in the Tamiḻ Grammar on the one hand, and the Kātantra and the like on the other.

A verb (as already said) is called in Tamiḻ viṇai which corresponds to kriyā. For the agreement to be complete some representative of ākhyāta should be used, but kriyā actually occurs in an explanatory sense[1], and is, therefore, probably the older term. The Tamiḻ verb differs essentially from the Sanskrit, and has only three tenses[2] with an imperative. The first are called niყaḻ-pŏḻuðu (now passing time), iṟanða-pŏḻuðu (past time) and ĕðir-pŏḻuðu (before time)[3]. The imperative is called eval or command[4]. These are obviously translations of varta-mānakāla, paroxakāla (or bhūtakāla) and bhavishyatkāla[5]; the Tamiḻ name for the imperative is from the Sanskrit anumati[6]. Verbs are called in Tamiḻ either ta*n*vi*n*ai (self-verb)[7] or piṟavi*n*ai (outward-verb), these terms are evidently translations of the Sanskrit ātmanepada and para-smaipada, but the distinction they mark in Tamiḻ might be better expressed, as these two classes of verbs correspond rather to intransitives and transitives.

Some of these terms also occur in Pāṇini, but, as in the case of those relating to nouns they are mentioned incidentally, and form no part of his system, which has entirely artificial words as names for tenses, composed of l, a vowel, and ṭ or ṇ. That Pāṇini explains these symbols by the simple Aindra terms shows that these last were commonly understood, and are, therefore, the older terms[8].

The Tamiḻ language is so entirely different from the Sanskrit that it is useless to look much further for technical grammatical terms be-

1) Kāt. iii., 1, 9. Ṛik. pr. xii., 8.

2) Tolk. ii., 6, 2.

3) Tolk. ii., 6, 3 and 44. Kāla is actually used for 'tense' in the Tolkāppiyam.

4) Not in the Tolkāppiyam apparently; it occurs in the Na*n*nūl.

5) Kāt. iii., 1, 11; 13: 15. Kacc. vi., 1, 8; 12; 17. For paroxā see Ath. pr. iv., 84. cfr. Mahābhāshya, f. 7 b. "traya*h* kālā*h* bhūta-bhavishyad vartamānā*h*".

6) Kāt. iii., 1, 18.

7) Tolk. ii., 6, 6.

8) *e. g.* P. iii., 2, 123: vartamāne laṭ; iii., 3, 3. bhavishyati gamyādaya*h*.

longing to the Aindra school. For example, the arrangement of the persons in the tenses includes masculine and feminine terminations (for human beings) and also neuter endings of the third person; this necessarily renders impossible an adherence to the Sanskrit model[1]. A few more terms may, however, be mentioned: 1. çāriyai[2] which is the name of letters inserted between a word and an affix; it is from √çār 'to resort to' or 'to come on,' and is thus the exact equivalent of the Sanskrit āgama[3]. 2. The term used in the Tolkāppiyam for the loss or elision of a letter is kĕḍuδal[4] from √kĕḍu 'to be destroyed or lost'; this is exactly the equivalent of lopa[5]. 3. In the same treatise we find mayakkam[6] used as the name of a group of consonants occurring together; this word is from √mayakku 'to confuse or attract' and it corresponds to the sa*m*yoga[7] of the corresponding Sanskrit treatises. Again we find īṟu[8] which answers to anta as generally used in the Sanskrit treatises.

The above comparison of the technical terms of the Tolkāppiyam on the one hand, and the Kātantra etc. on the other, will, I think, establish the general identity of system of all these grammars, as I have already stated[9]. The comparison (to a limited extent) with the terms used by Pāṇini prove that these last are far more artificial and precise and, therefore, more recent than the former. The relation of the two is just the same as that between the mediæval notation of algebraic problems and the modern system. Where, for example, Cardan wrote 'cosa' and 'census' we now put x and x^2 [10]. So where the Aindra Grammars have an ordinary word used in a technical sense, Pāṇini mostly has a mere symbol[11]. If the series of technical terms that I have just discussed be

1) The name of the personal terminations of verbs is vibhakti (Kacc. vi., 1). The Kātantra does not use this word in a sūtra, but the commentators assume it. The Tolkāppiyam, on the other hand, prohibits vēṟṟumai (vibhakti) to verbs (ii., 6, 1), and restricts this term solely to nouns, no doubt, because the personal terminations to the verbs are at once recognized as pronouns.

2) Tolk. i., 6, 1.

3) Kāt. ii., 1, 6; Kacc. i., 4, 6; Ṛik. pr. ii., 11; Taitt. pr. i, 23; Atharva pr. iii., 78; Kāty. pr. i., 187.

4) Tolk. i., 4, 18 and 20; 5, 15 and 18 etc.

5) Ṛik. pr. iv., 7; Taitt. pr.. i., 56; Atharva pr. i., 67; Kāt. i., 2, 1; Kacc. i., 2, 1.

6) Tolk. i., 2, 14.

7) Ṛik. pr. (i., 7). Taitt. pr. xxi., 4. Atharva pr. i., 51.

8) Tolk. i., 2, 6 and 38 etc.

9) Above pp. 11-12.

10) Morley's "Jerome Cardan" i., p. 222.

11) There are a few anubandhas in the Kātantra etc., but these must be considered further on.

considered, it will clearly be seen that the terms used in the Tolkāppiyam, Kātantra, and Kaccāyana all hang together as parts of one system, and that the resemblance holds good throughout. Thus the similarity in the technical terms regarding phonetics is not varied when we come to inflection, and several terms which can find no place in the Tamil grammar occur in the others[1]; for these reasons it is safe to presume that the Prātiçākhyas all belong to the same school, though they do not go beyond phonetics, and so far their evidence is defective.

I shall now collect the conventional (technical) terms discussed above, giving, firstly, the term used in the Tolkāppiyam in its original Sanskrit form, if possible[2], and marked *. Variations are included in ( ) following, the source being indicated. Those words which also occur in Pāṇini[3] are marked by **thick type**, and additional words not in the Tolkāppiyam but which occur in all or most of the Grammars that I now have classed together, are in spaced type.

aghoshavat
* aniṅgya (in Prātiçākhyas)
anunāsika
* anumati
anushaṅga (not in the Prātiçākhyas)
anusvāra
* **anta**
* **antaḥstha**
ākhyāta
* āgama
* **ātmanepada**
* āmantrita *or* āmantraṇa
* iṅgya (in Prātiçākhyas)
** iḍaiššol (nipāta in all the others)
upadhā
upadhmānīya
upasarga
** urіššol (upasarga, in all the others)
ūshman
ekavacana
* -kāra
* kāla
* kriyā (akhyāta, in all the others)
guṇa
ghoshavat
jihvāmūlīya
* **dīrgha**
* **dvitīyā** etc.[4]
dhātu (used by Yāska and, before him, by Çākaṭāyana)
dvivacana
* nāman

1) *e. g.* upadhā. Kāt. i., 4, 7; Kacc. Liṅga (=Pāṇini's prātipadika); Kāt. ii., 1, 1; Kacc. ii., 1, 2. Pravāda is the term in the Ṛik. pr. (ii., 39). Prof. Max Müller noticed (in his A. S. Literature) that Pāṇini was the first to distinguish the genders for which he uses this word. Anushaṅga, Kāt. ii., 1, 12. Ṛik. pr. ii., 18; Atharva pr. i., 92. Kāty. pr. i., 35.

2) The two that cannot be re-translated are marked * *

3) *i. e.* in the sūtras of Pāṇini *only*, I do not include the vārttikas etc.

4) I omit tṛitīyā and the other names of cases up to saptamī.

nāmin (bhāvin in the Kāty. pr.)
nipāta
* pada
pararūpa
* parasmaipada
paroxakāla (*or* bhūtakāla)
prakṛiti (cfr. Kāt.)
pratyaya
* prathamā
pradhāna
* prayatna
bahuvacana
* bhavishyatkāla
* bhūtakāla
* mātrā
liṅga (not in Pāṇini with the same sense; = pravāda in Prātiçākhyas)
* lōpa
* varga
varṇa (in Pāṇini, i., 1, 9 in savarṇa only)
* vartamānakāla
vikṛiti
* vibhakti
visarjanīya or visarga
vṛiddhi
vyañjana
* saṁyoga
* sandhi
sandhyaxara
samāna (*i. e.* varṇa)
samāsa
savarṇa
* sthāna
* sparça
* svara (originally = vowel or accent. Pāṇini has it in the last sense only)
* hrasva

In the above list I have purposely excluded varṇa and axara as these terms, though common to the Sanskrit treatises, are not represented in the Tamiḻ which has ĕḻuttu in their place, a word that can be best translated by likhita. As I have shown elsewhere[1], there are strong reasons for believing that the Tamiḻ people had an independent system of writing in use before their language was analysed by grammarians from the North. The terms relating to samāsa are older than Pāṇini, but do not occur in the Tamiḻ Grammar.

Thus, as far as these terms go, it is clear that if we find almost any one of them in any treatise, we are certain to find the rest in due course; but this is not the case if we take Pāṇini's grammar. I have already given several instances which show the great development in the system of technical terms as used by the last, compared with the former; I shall now show that Pāṇini's use of the Aindra terms proves that they belong to an older system, and that they probably belong to the system of the grammarians whom he occasionally quotes as "Prāñcaḥ".

1) "Elements of S. Indian Palæography", p. 48.

The late Profr. Goldstücker (who first, perhaps, in Europe, mastered the intricate system of Pāṇini's grammar) pointed out that the rules contained in the sūtras i., 2, 53—57 explain the innovations made by Pāṇini as regards the technical terms used by his predecessors in the science. Goldstücker's conclusions are[1]:

I. "That his (*i. e.* Pāṇini's) grammar does not treat of those sa*n*jñās or conventional names which are known and settled otherwise.

II. "That this term sa*n*jñā must be understood in our (*i. e.* Pāṇini's) rule to concern only such conventional names as have an etymology.

III. "That it applies also to grammatical terms which admit of an etymology, but not to those which are merely grammatical symbols.

IV. "That such terms as ṭi, ghu and bha were known and settled before Pāṇini's grammar, but that, nevertheless, they are defined by Pāṇini, because they are not etymological terms"[2]. Pāṇini himself (i., 2, 56) gives examples, viz. pradhāna and pratyaya which are, therefore, older than his system.

Now if one examines Pāṇini's sūtras narrowly, it becomes evident that there are certain terms which he always uses without a definition and which belong to the Aindra school, whereas he gives definitions of certain others which belong to the same school, but which he uses in a modified sense and not as they were originally used.

Firstly, as regards Aindra terms which Pāṇini uses without a definition. These are prathamā, dvitīyā, tṛitīyā, caturthī, pañcamī, shashṭhī and saptamī as names of cases[3]. Why Pāṇini uses these terms is evident; had he restricted himself to his own symbols, his meaning would not have appeared at all[4] in these particular sūtras, and thus he was compelled to use the older terms or sacrifice his principle of the utmost possible conciseness of expression. The Commentary to the original Calcutta edition, and which is a compilation from earlier similar works, states in more than one place that these names of cases are technical terms of the 'prāñca*h*' grammarians. Thus, on P. ii., 3, 13, in which caturthī oc-

1) "Pāṇini's Place" (sep. imp.) p. 166.

2) I shall discuss this view in due course, further on, when I shall attempt to determine Pāṇini's innovations.

3) See the Index at the end of the second volume of Böhtlingk's edition of Pāṇini for the places where these terms occur.

4) For these sūtras refer to the meaning of some expressions, and not to the grammatical form.

curs, this term is explained by: "caturthī 'ti sanjñā prācām". Again on sūtra ii., 3, 46, in which prathamā occurs, the same explanation is given. It is unlikely that this statement is without authority, but what that authority is, I have as yet failed to discover, though I have examined the Kāçikā vṛitti and other most likely sources, for this statement. It has been accepted by Böhtlingk and Goldstücker, however, but without indication of the authority on which it rests[1]; yet considering the nature of the grammatical teaching given in India, and its absolute reliance on, and servile imitation of the authorities, such a statement can hardly have been made without reason, and, therefore, must not be wholly rejected. The other Aindra terms used by Pāṇini without a definition are: anusvāra; anta; ekavacana, dvivacana and bahuvacana (of nouns); upasarga; nipāta; dhātu; pratyaya; pradhāna; prayatna; bhavishyat (-kāla); vartamāna (-kāla). Besides these one must add nearly all the terms relating to samāsa, but I shall not discuss them as they naturally cannot be found in Tamiḻ. Thus it is certain that Pāṇini found these conventional terms already in use, and generally understood.

The Aindra terms of which Pāṇini apparently gives definitions are as follows: anunāsika; ātmanepada; āmantrita; upadhā; guṇa; dīrgha; pada; parasmaipada; vibhakti; vṛiddhi; sa*m*yoga; savarṇa; hrasva. But it by no means necessarily follows that Pāṇini invented or first used these terms, for, (as I shall now proceed to show), he has in many cases improved and made more exact the use of an old term and in other cases his system required a new definition.

Anunāsika. Pāṇini defines this term in i., 1, 8—"mukhanāsikāvacano 'nunāsika*h*." In the Prātiçākhyas anunāsika is the name of the nasals ṅ, ń, ṇ, etc. and certain other letters in certain positions; here, in Pāṇini, we find a physiological explanation which supersedes the enumeration of particular cases in the earlier books.

---

1) See Böhtlingk's edition (ii., p. 487, s. v. dvitīyā): "Die Endungen des 2ten Casus bei den östlichen Grammatikern" cfr. also the passage on p. xii. of the same volume: "Es kommen nämlich in seinem Werke für mehrere grammatische Elemente doppelte Kunstausdrücke vor, von denen der eine ihm selbst eigen ist, der andere dagegen, nach dem Zeugnisse seiner Commentatoren, von den östlichen Grammatikern entlehnt ist." Goldstücker ("Pāṇini's Place" p. 167 of the sep. imp.) says: "And the commentators apprise us that these words (*i. e.* prathamā, etc.) were technical names used by the eastern grammarians which are referred to by Pāṇini in some of his rules". The sources from which the Commentary in the Calcutta edition was taken are mentioned on the title-page. Prof. Weber has identified the Kātyāyanīya Prātiçākhya with the Prācya School, and Goldstücker (*u. s.* p. 217) classes the Phiṭ sūtras with the same. The last has only partially the Aindra terms. (See also Kielhorn's edition p. 11.)

Ātmanepada etc. Pāṇini (i., 4, 99) says: "la*h* parasmaipadam"; in the next sūtra he defines ātmanepada—"taṅānāv ātmanepadam". In the Kātantra and Kaccāyana, these words are the name of certain terminations[1]; here symbols unknown to the earlier works are used, and new definitions are, therefore, necessary.

Āmantrita *or* āmantraṇa. Pāṇini (ii., 3, 48) says: "sā 'mantritam." This is no real definition, but is merely explanatory.

Upadhā. Pāṇini (i., 1, 65) says: "alo 'ntyāt pūrva upadhā." This definition differs but very little from that in the older system[2], but this slight change makes very plain the difference between Pāṇini's system and that followed by his predecessors; it is the first word ala*h*. The reason for this addition is given in the Mahābhāshya[3] viz. to avoid making it apply to the indicatory suffixes. In the older treatises this precaution was unnecessary, for they did not use such symbols at all, if we may infer decisively from the Prātiçākhyas and Tolkāppiyam, and there are very few such in the Kātantra and in Kaccāyana's Grammar[4].

Guṇa. In the old treatises guṇa occurs, but a new definition was necessary in Pāṇini's Grammar, as he uses the Çiva-sūtras; he defines it accordingly by a pratyāhāra.

Dīrgha and hrasva. The old definition was by mātrās; Pāṇini (i., 2, 27) gives a new conventional value: "ū 3 kālo 'j jhrasvadīrghapluta*h*".

Pada. This is again defined by Pāṇini (i., 4, 14): "suptiṅanta*m* padam"; but the definition is obviously necessary as sup and tiṅ are unknown to the earlier works. The definition in the Kātantra[5] is: "pūrvaparayor arthopalabdhau padam".

Lopa. Pāṇini (i., 1, 69) says: "adarçana*m* lopa*h*". This is really a new definition, or rather the first; for, elsewhere, the word is simply used in its ordinary sense without explanation. It evidently refers to written symbols, and Pāṇini was probably the first grammarian who wrote his treatise. He also uses some new terms—lu and luk, lup, çlu.

---

1) Kāt. iii., 1, 1-2. Kacc. p. 221.

2) Kāt. (ii., 1, 11)—"antyāt pūrva upadhā". Atharva pr. i., 92; Kāty. pr. i., 85.

3) Mahābh. (Ed. Benares, i., fol. 160, *b.*), "Kim idam algrahaṇam antyaviçeshaṇam? eva*m* bhavitum arhati | upadhāsa*n*jñāyām algrahaṇam antyanirdeçaç ce 'tsaṅghātapratishedha*h* |" etc.

4) It is to be noticed that this definition (in the form "varṇād antyāt pūrva upadhā") occurs in the Atharva pr. (i., 92) and in the Kātyāyanīya pr. (i., 85). Profr. Whitney remarks that in the Ṛik pr. upadhā has a more general signification (p. 59 of his edition of the Atharva pr.). The Taitt. pr. (as Profr. Whitney points out) has not this term.

5) Kāt. i., 1, 20. The C. explains "pūrvaparayo*h*" by "prakṛitivibhaktayo*h*."

Vibhakti. Pāṇini (i., 4, 104) defines this term: "vibhaktiç ca". This sūtra is intended to declare that sup and tiṅ are called vibhakti. In the older books the mere list of terminations was given, here the introduction of the symbols sup and tiṅ renders explanation necessary.

Vṛiddhi. The reason for this fresh definition is the same as in the case of guṇa.

Sa*m*yoga. Here again the use of the Çiva-sūtras renders a new definition necessary (i., 1, 7)—"halo 'nantarā*h* sa*m*yoga*h*". The old definition (Ṛik. pr. i., 7) is: "sa*m*yogo vyañjanasannipāta*h* which would not suit the new term for consonants.

Savarṇa. This is not defined in the older books, but Pāṇini sums up all their researches on the nature of alphabetic sounds by—"tulyāsyaprayatna*m* savarṇam" (i., 1, 9)—a definition which completely supersedes the old lists of analogous letters.

Thus of the Aindra terms used by Pāṇini, he uses the greater number without definition, and they are, therefore, to be considered as in use before his time, and this result follows from his own rule[1]. A somewhat smaller number of Aindra terms he does define, but it is plain that he does not use these terms in their old sense, or else that a new and more precise definition is necessary in consequence of the system of technical symbols used by him, and by which the old idea is expressed in a new way. These last instances thus do not fall under his rule, and it does not, in consequence, follow that he invented these terms.

In making this comparison, I have, as already said, noticed only the sūtras of Pāṇini; it is little likely that these can have been tampered with or improved to any serious extent, but the case is different with the subordinate literature such as the Gaṇapāṭha etc. The vārttikas and Patañjali's commentary, as we have them, contain a large number of Aindra terms (*e. g.* svara and vyañjana) which do not occur in Pāṇini, and considering the nature of these texts and their object, viz., to respectively correct and rehabilitate Pāṇini, their presence is evidence in favour of the view taken above. If (as has been explained above) the Commentators are right in identifying the Aindra terms for cases as those of the Prāñca*h*, the opinions of those grammarians as quoted by Pāṇini should correspond with the works which I have shown to belong to the Aindra school. Now Pāṇini quotes these grammarians in eight sūtras[2].

1) i., 2, 53 ffg.

2) iii., 4, 18; iv., 1, 17. 43. 160; v., 3, 80. 94. 4, 101; viii., 2, 86.

The first of these is: "alaṅkhalvoḥ pratishedhayoḥ prācām ktvā", and this sūtra actually occurs in the Kātantra[1] with the omission of prācām; what is here taught is, therefore, the doctrine of the school to which the Kātantra belongs. The next three sūtras referred to treat of the formation of certain feminine nouns, but I cannot trace any similarity in them, nor in respect of the remaining sūtras. Considering the nature of the books we have for comparison, and that of the complete treatises one is in Pāli and the other in Tamiḻ both of which necessarily allow of only a limited adaptation of the original system, and that rather in form than in matter, this nearly negative result is all that could be expected, and does not really affect the question.

Whether the identity of the Aindra School with the Prāñcaḥ that Pāṇini quotes be admitted or not, it seems to me that it is impossible generally to translate this name any longer by "Eastern Grammarians", and that the only satisfactory rendering is "Former Grammarians". Pāṇini does occasionally use the ambiguous term prāñc[2] in a geographical sense, but only where the words he refers to, are geographical. In the sūtras where he mentions the grammatical doctrine of the prāñcaḥ, the Commentators (*e. g.* the Kāçikā vṛitti) always explain the word prācām by prācām ācāryāṇām matena, and as we now know that Pāṇini was a native of

---

1) vi., 1. It adds, however, vā and makes it optional.

2) Prāñc and its derivatives mean both *a*) 'former' or 'old', and also *b*) 'eastern' in all periods of Sanskrit Literature. A few examples will make this plain:

a. "Sarvadarçanassaṅgraha" (p. 122): "Asya praçnasya prativacanam p r ā c y ā m mīmāṁsāyām pradarçi Jaimininā muninā".

"Paribhāshenduçekhara", introduction, p. i. (of Dr. Kielhorn's admirable edition): "Prācīnavyākaraṇatantre vācanikāny atra Pāṇinīyatantre jñāpakanyāyasiddhāni bhāshyavārttikayor nibaddhāni yāni paribhāshārūpāni tāni vyākhyāyante". Vaidyanātha (in his C. on this text) explains that the grammarians who preceded Pāṇini were Indra and the like.

Bhaṭṭoji Dīxita's "Siddhāntakaumudī (Calcutta edition of 1870, vol. ii., p. 188) "Sarve paxāḥ prācām granthe sthitāḥ". This refers to the Prakriyākaumudī and the plural 'prācām' is honorific; there could not have well been many authors to one book. Elsewhere in the S. K., Bhaṭṭoji refers to the same treatise as 'Prācīnaprakriyā'. So also in his Prauḍhamanoramā he means the Prakriyākaumudī of Rāmacandra and his followers where he mentions the 'prāñcaḥ' or 'prācīnaprakriyā' which he always does with censure.

b. But, on the other hand, even Pāṇini uses the word also with the sense of 'Eastern' (cfr. i., 1, 75), and it is not unusual in this sense in grammatical works. So Xīrasvāmin (in his Commentary on the Amarakosha, i., 1, 1, 1) says: "'tripishṭapam' iti prācyāḥ prāyeṇa hy ete pa(b)au çasau ca vyatyasasya paṭhanti". This clearly refers to the Eastern or Bengali pronunciation, as the actual pronunciation jība (for jīva) and saṇa (for çaṇa) prove. [Profr. Aufrecht has lately described the I. O. MS. of Xīrasvāmin in the Zeitschrift d. d. M-G. xxviii., pp. 103 ffg. I have only a defective MS. (Tanjore, No. 5,580) to refer to, and this differs in many places from Profr. Aufrecht's quotations; *e. g.* in i., 1, 1, 30 there is no mention of the

4

Çālātura[1], a glance at the map will show that a geographical meaning cannot possibly be given to the word. It must also be taken into consideration that even if Pāṇini could have referred to some of his predecessors as 'Eastern', yet that such a term could not possibly be continued (as we find is the case) by his successors (*e.g.* Patañjali) many of whom lived to the south-east of Pāṇini's native place; they would rather have mentioned them by name.

In an enquiry of this nature small details of corroborative evidence are not to be neglected, and it is, thus, necessary to remark that the grammatical terms which are found in the Vedic works are Aindra terms. There can be no doubt that these words (as used by Grammarians) are older than Pāṇini, for this reason; as, though, no doubt, the chronology of the Vedic literature is beset with difficulties, the matter, at least of the books I am going to quote, can be safely put down as anterior to Pāṇini; such passages[2] can hardly have been interpolated for any conceivable reason.

The first passage occurs in the Taittirīya or first Upanishad of the Taittirīya Āraṇyaka (vii., 1, 2)[3]; it runs: çixā*m* vyākhyāsyāma*h* | varṇā*h* svara*h* | mātrā balam | sāma santāna*h* | ity ukta*h* çixādhyāya*h* ||

We find here merely the bare heads of matter to be treated in a phonetical compendium such as the çixās now actually in existence in considerable numbers, but varṇa, svara and mātrā are actually Aindra terms.

---

paççātyā*h*, but only the prācyā*h* are referred to. Again in iii., 3, 20 only the udīcyā*h* are referred to.] Again in the Bhela Sa*m*hitā (*a.* xiii., 8) we find this word used in the sense of 'Eastern people' or Natives of Bengal (?):

Matsyānnabhojino nitya*m* prācyā*h* syu*h* kaphapittina*h* |
Çlīpada*m* galagaṇḍa*m* ca prāyaças teshu dṛiçyate ||

But it is sufficient to point out the ambiguity of the word and that no general rule can be given as to its rendering. The possible meanings in Pāṇini appear to be *a*) former (grammarians), *b*) former (use of the language). To these udac appears as a contrast viz., in the sense of 'recent'. Pāṇini, in short, recognizes historical development in Sanskrit. To the natural objection—if Pāṇini's predecessors are called prāñca*h* collectively by him, why then does he quote individual authors?—the explanation appears to me to be easy and satisfactory, viz., if he refers to a peculiar doctrine in which all his predecessors were agreed, he mentions them collectively as Prāñca*h*; if however he refers to individual differences, he names his authority.

1) Near Attock. See Cunningham's "Ancient Geography of India" i., pp. 57-8.

2) The three first passages have already been noticed by Profr. Max Müller (A. S. Lit. p. 160, 2nd ed.) as containing grammatical terms. In this he follows Profr. Weber ("Indische Studien" iv., p. 76).

3) Bibl. Indica edition (by Rājendralāl Mitra) p. 725. It is useless to give here the interpretations of the numerous Commentators, for they add really nothing; the sense of the passage is plain enough.

The Chāndogya Upanishad[1] mentions sparça, svara and ūshman which are all Aindra terms also.

In the Çatapatha Brāhmaṇa[2] we find: Ne 'd ekavacanena bahuvacanam vyavāyāme 'ti. We have already seen that ekavacana and bahuvacana are Aindra terms. In the Aitareya Brāhmaṇa axara, axarapaṅkti, caturaxara, varṇa, -kāra and pada[3] occur; these belong to the same class of terms. Though few, they imply an advanced analysis of words.

The most important passage from this stand-point is, however, one in the relatively late Gopatha Brāhmaṇa (i., 24). It runs: "Oṃkāram pṛicchāmaḥ ko dhātuḥ kiṃ prātipadikam kiṃ nāmā 'khyātam kiṃ liṅgam kiṃ vacanam kā vibhaktiḥ kaḥ pratyayaḥ kaḥ svara upasargo nipātaḥ kiṃ vai vyākaraṇam ko vikāraḥ ko vikārī katimātraḥ kativarṇaḥ katyaxaraḥ katipadaḥ kaḥ saṃyogaḥ kiṃ sthānānupradānakaraṇam çixukāḥ kim uccārayanti kiṃ chandaḥ ko varṇa iti pūrve praçnāḥ"[4]. This short passage contains all the chief Aindra terms, but it is by no means the only one in this Brāhmaṇa in which grammatical terms occur[5]. It is useless to refer to the Tāṇḍya and other Brāhmaṇas of the Sāma Veda as in these many grammatical terms (*e. g.* vibhakti) are used in a different technical sense and refer to the Sāma chants.

Profr. Weber has already noticed[6] the grammatical terms which occur in the Vedic (kalpa) sūtras and these (vyañjana; okāra; makāra; tālusthāna; oshṭyasthāna; pluta; trimātra; sandhyaxara; pragṛihya (in the Çāṅkhāyanasūtra); nāmam (in the Kātyāyanasūtra) also belong to the Aindra School. Those in the Gṛihya sūtras (which are probably later) are of a mixed character, but for the most part they and the works based on them preserve the older terms[7].

This result is considerable, as the many terms actually occurring in Vedic works are Aindra terms, and the absence of the least trace of any

1) Dr. Roer's edition (in the Bibl. Indica) p. 135 (p. ii., 22, 3—5).

2) Edited by Dr. A. Weber p. 990. In a note on p. 1018 Profr. Weber shows that at the time this Brāhmaṇa was written, grammar had advanced far enough to identify roots such as √bhū and √as. This is supported by many passages in the Aitareya Br. (*ed.* Haug)—i., 10; ii., 1; iii., 2 and 29 (√mad), 39 and 47 (sudhā identified with suhita); iv., 6. 29. 32; v., 5 (janūmahi is said to be jāta-vat) etc.

3) Ed. Profr. Haug, P. i., 5; ii., 24; v., 3; etc.

4) I have taken the Bibl. Indica text which I have collated with Tanjore 2,528. This last omits 'kaḥ pratyayaḥ'.

5) *e. g.* axara (i., 16); dvivarṇa (do.); varṇa (do.); caturmātra (do.); akāra (i., 20); ekāxara (i., 22) etc.

6) "Indische Studien" iv., p. 75 *note*.

7) *e. g.* by Mānavadharmaçāstra ii., 33, a woman's name is to be dīrghavarṇānta.

other systems of conventional terms forming part of a grammatical system, clearly shows that the Aindra system is the oldest.

Again a comparison of the style of composition of the Kātantra, Kaccāyana's Grammar, the Prātiçākhyas and the Tolkāppiyam on the one hand and that of Pāṇini on the other, shows an immense development in every way. As far as the differentiation and specialization of the technical terms is concerned, I have already given some examples[1]. The brevity of Pāṇini's sūtras is well known, and the involved arrangement which he has adopted, perplexes even old students[2], on the other hand the Kātantra and similar books present no difficulty worth mentioning[3]. Regnier describes, very aptly, the style of the Ṛigvedaprātiçākhya in the following terms: "La méthode du Prātiçākhya dans ces trois chapitres (vii., viii., ix), comme presque partout ailleurs, est tout empirique. Il se contente généralement d'énumérer les faits, sans en chercher la raison, et le petit nombre de règles qu'il établit ne sont fondées, à fort peu d'exceptions près, que sur des rencontres et des combinaisons fortuites, ou sur des analogies toutes mécaniques qui ne s'expliquent, en général, que par la liberté que cet antique idiome laissait au poëte, en ce qui touche à la quantité". The other three Prātiçākhyas are more modern in style and arrangement, especially the ones belonging to the white Yajur and to the Atharva Vedas[4]; but in these respects they are nevertheless a great contrast to Pāṇini's Grammar. Compared with it the style in which they are written is simple. They want however the paribhāshās and similar explanations, and in this respect resemble Pāṇini and the later

1) Above pp. 13, 15, 17, 19 *note* 1, 28.

2) This will be easily seen by taking the Calcutta edition of the Siddāntakaumudī and observing how in any chapter (*e. g.* inflection of nouns or verbs) the sūtras come indifferently from all parts of Pāṇini's text.

3) Aufrecht ("Catalogus" p. 169) says: "Hac enumeratione singulas grammaticæ (*i. e.* Kātantræ) partes certa quadam satisque justa ratione dispositas esse vides. Regulæ ipsæ vel sine commentario perspicuæ sunt, neque ea brevitate et obscuritate laborant, quibus Pāṇini, ejusque schola studuerunt". These words apply equally to Kaccāyana's Grammar which is almost a counterpart of the Kātantra, as already shown.

4) Profr. Whitney (Atharva pr. p. 247) says: "It may be said that our treatise is much more curt and concise, and more ready to pass without notice what may be assumed as already known, than either of the others. Definitions of terms are far from numerous, and the whole department of p a r i b h ā s h ā, or explanation of modes of phraseology, of extent, bearing, and application of the rules and the like, which in all the other Prātiçākhyas occupies considerable space, is here almost wanting. This is in part owing to the simpler and less artificial mode of arrangement adopted in our work." The Kāt. pr. has some Pāṇinean terms, *e. g.* tiṅ; Goldstücker ("Pāṇini's Place", pp. 200 ffg.) has already given reasons for believing that this treatise is in its present state posterior to Pāṇini.

grammars[1], and show that they have not preserved their primitive forms in all particulars.

A few examples will make this plain as regards the style of the several works; the development of the technical terms used by Pāṇini has already been sufficiently exemplified, as well as the several arrangements of matter.

The want of the Çivasūtras and the consequent absence of pratyāhāras in the works I have grouped together as belonging to the Aindra School, cause a marked difference of style in these as compared with Pāṇini. This difference can be easily grasped if the rules referring to the sandhi of diphthongs be compared. In Pāṇini this is done by a single rule[2]—"eco 'yavāyāvaḥ", in which (it is hardly necessary to remark) 'ec' stands for e (o, ṅ, ai, au) c as we find in the Çivasūtras. To express this same rule in the Kātantra four sūtras or rules[3] are necessary, "e ay; ai āy; o av; au ār." The same is the case in the rules regarding the sandhi of consonants. The works I have grouped together as belonging to the Aindra school, all agree in this respect with the Kātantra, wherever they have to enumerate a series of letters all the letters are mentioned, and are not expressed by a pratyāhāra as in Pāṇini[4]. But in the last we find the system carried much further and used to express collectively a number of terminations which can be grouped together, *e. g.* tiṅ stands for the 9 terminations (of the parasmaipada verb) -ti to -nti. In the Aindra works all these are severally enumerated.

Again the simplicity of the Aindra treatises[5] is very apparent in the absence of gaṇas (or a single word of a class followed by another meaning 'and the like' to indicate all the words of the class to which a rule or rules apply), but which exist in Pāṇini's grammar in such numbers[6]. Profr. Whitney's remarks[7] must be quoted here. He says: "The form of statement (*i. e.* gaṇa) is characteristic of the Atharva prātiçākhya[8] and

1) Cfr. the extract already given from Kielhorn's "Paribhāshenduçekhara" (above p. 25).

2) P. vi., 1, 78.

3) Kāt. i, 2, 12-15.

4) Cfr. Kacc. 1, 4, 6, etc.; Ṛik. pr. introductory lines and 1, 8-12; Atharva pr. i, 41 and 58 etc.; Taitt. pr. 1, 31 etc.; Kāty. pr. 1, 65 and 66 etc.; Tolk. i., 1, 3. (="Of those letters five a, i, u, ĕ, ŏ are......short"); 4 (= "Seven ā, ī, ū, e, o, ai, au are......long") etc.

5) Except the Atharva prātiçākhya which is the most artificial in arrangement of all, though as a scientific treatise it is, in consequence, much simpler and more complete. Whitney (Ath. pr.) p. 248.

6) There are about 300 in Pāṇini's Grammar. See Böhtlingk's edition, vol. II. where most are given.

7) Atharva pr. 1, 65 (p. 48).

8) In the Ath. pr. there are about 24 gaṇas.

of Pāṇini, and of them only. The Vāj. Pr. employs it but once (v. 38), the others not at all (Ṛ. pr. iv., 39, where, for convenience's sake, a list is thus referred to in one verse which is given in full in the next, furnishes but one accidental and insignificant analogy)." The Taittirīya Prātiçākhya does not give any satisfactory proof of the use of gaṇas, as only three occur (v., 40, Çaityāyanādi; xxiii., 11, mandrādi; xxiv., 4, axarasaṁhitādi), none of which are real gaṇas or lists of words unconnected except so far as they come under a rule, and the two last belong to parts of the treatise which are supposed to be additions[1]. The Tolkāppiyam is also wanting in gaṇas though they occur in the more recent Naṉṉūl[2]. The Kātantra and Kaccāyana exhibit very few such gaṇas.

The natural conclusion is that gaṇas were hardly used by the Aindra grammarians, and there are signs that Pāṇini was the first to use them extensively even if he did not invent the system[3]. Yet again, the comparison of the subject matter is of importance. It has been repeatedly noticed that some of the Prātiçākhyas contain irrelevant matter, and this is also the case with the Tolkāppiyam[4]. In the last, besides the strictly grammatical part, the elements of rhetoric and metre, also observations on the method of teaching are given. So in the Ṛigveda Prātiçākhya the 15th chapter is a description of the method followed in a Vedic school, and chapters 16, 17 and 18 are on prosody. The Atharva and Kātyāyanīya Prātiçākhyas include recommendations of Vedic study[5]. It is obvious that this inclusion of irrelevant matter is a characteristic of primitive treatises composed before grammar, etymology, prosody, and exegesis had been differentiated; a state of things that we find in the Brāhmaṇas where we must look for the beginning of Indian science. In these, metrical observations abound, and show that attention was paid very early to metres. In fact a fairly complete system of prosody could be gathered from the Brāhmaṇas though they only display the elements of grammar and etymology[6]: and so far the older Sanskrit grammars agree

1) See Profr. Whitney's remarks on p. 432 of his edition.

2) In the Naṉṉūl mudal is used as the equivalent of ādi.

3) For example he has three ways of expressing a gaṇa: 1) by ādi added to the first word of the class; 2) by prabhṛiti added to the first word; 3) by the first word being put in the plural form.

4) Tolk. iii., 9. cfr. Naṉṉūl, i.

5) Atharva pr. iv., 101-109. Kāty. pr. i., 20-26, viii., 32-34 and 35-42. Taitt. pr. xxiv., 5-6.

6) Cfr. Ait. Br. Gopathabr. etc. passim Profr. Max Müller has remarked on the etymological parts in his Ancient Sanskrit Literature (ed. 2), p. 158. See also Devatādhyāya Brāhmaṇa, § 3, and my preface (p. v.) in which this passage is compared with a passage in Yāska (p. 119 of Roth's edition).

with the nature of the earliest grammar-studies of the Greeks. Mr. Sayce says of the labours of the Sophists before Dionysius Thrax that they resulted in "a rough classification of the principal parts of speech for the purposes of oratorical study; but without the contrast afforded by another language these classifications could not but remain confused with rhetoric and devoid of all method and thorough-going arrangement"[1].

Thus from whatever point of view—arrangement, technical terms, style of composition or contents—we may consider the Aindra treatises (as I term them), it is plain that, though they differ in some respects between themselves, they represent a school of grammar older than that of Pāṇini. It would be interesting to compare the differences, which I have more than once noticed, but these are special niceties of grammar as applied to the texts used by different Vedic schools or çākhās[2] and do not belong to the science of grammar as understood in a general sense. It would, therefore, be unsafe to draw any conclusions from them even were the ascriptions of special doctrines to individual grammarians entirely beyond doubt. But this is not the case, and the reason for it is apparent: hardly any work belonging to the older or middle Sanskrit literature has escaped extensive rehandling and interpolation; the Aindra treatises belong to a system older than Pāṇini's, though there is perhaps reason to believe that not one of them is, as a whole, older than the grammar of the last. The influences under which these successive redactions were made have yet to be traced, but I shall give sufficient proof that they have been made[3]. Pāṇini's grammar has, in all probability, been little tampered with; we have better warrant for its integrity than in the case of any other work, but it would be premature to assert that it is absolutely intact. Yet, as it is, it furnishes a safe standard of comparison, and the result is against the texts of the Prātiçākhyas as we have them, and, above all, against the Çākaṭāyana Grammar.

It follows from the preceding enquiry that by the Aindra Grammar one must understand a school of grammar, and not a specific work by an individual; and if the passages in which the Aindra Grammar is mentioned, and which I have collected above be examined closely, it

---

1) "Principles of Comparative Philology" p. 246.

2) Yāska's "Nirukta" (Naig. i. 17): "padaprakṛitīni sarvacaraṇānām pārshadāni". The remarks of Professors Goldstücker and Whitney are already given on p. 9 *note* 4. See also Profr. Whitney's "Or. Studies" i., p. 72. Ūvaṭa Bhaṭṭa calls the Ṛikpr. a Pārshada.

3) See Appendix.

will be seen that they really bear this meaning, and do not attribute an actual grammatical treatise to the god Indra. Thus Kātyāyana is made to talk of "my Aindra Grammar", and the Tolkāppiyam is "according to the Aindra (system)". Indra was fabled to have originated the science of grammar, but the Indra (or Aiudra) Grammar was the primitive grammatical science as handed down by various teachers. Of these it is possible to draw up a considerable list of more or less certain names which I shall now give as complete as I can, leaving the consideration of existing works of the school to the end of this monograph, though I shall mark the names of those to whom existing books are attributed with a †.

Āgniveçya, T.
Āgniveçyāyana, T.
Āgrāyaṇa, N.
Ātreya, T. Tamiḻ CC.
Ānyatareya, Ṛik. pr.
Āpiçali, P. Mh. Bh.
Āhvarakas, T.
Ukhya, T.
Uttamottarīyas, T.
Udīcyas, (*i. e.* some of the individuals named in this list.)
Audumbarāyaṇa, N.
Aupamanyava, N.
Aupaçivi, K.
Aurṇavābha, N.
Kāṇḍamāyana, T.
Kāṇva, K.
Kātthakya, N.
Kāçakṛitsna, Mh. Bh.
Kāçyapa, K. T.
Kuṇara-Vāḍava, Mh. Bh.
Kauṇḍinya, T. (Sthavira K.)
Kautsa, Ṛik. pr.
Kauhalīputra, T.
Kroshtrīyā*h*, Mh. Bh.
Kraushṭuki, N.
Gārgya, Ṛik. pr. K. P.
Gālava, N. P.
Gonardīya (? = Patañjali) Mh. Bh.
† Gautama, T. (Gautamīyas) Mh. Bh.
Carmaçiras, N.
Cākravarmaṇa, P.
Jātūkarṇya, K.
Taitīki, N.
Taittirīyakas, T.
Dālbhya, K.
Pañcālas, Ṛik. pr.
Paushkarasādi, T. P. (vārtt.)
Prācyas, P. (*i. e.* some of the individuals named here.)
Plāxāyaṇa, T.
Plāxi, T.
Bāḍabhīkāra, T. (or Vāḍabhīkāra)
Bābhravya Kramakṛit, Ṛik. pr.
† Bhāradvāja, Ṛik. pr. T. (Bhāradvājīyas) Mh. Bh.
† Māṇḍukeya, Ṛik. pr.
Mācakīya, T.
Mīmā*m*sakas, T.
† Yāska, Ṛik. pr. T. Mh. Bh.
Vātsapra, T.

Vātsya (Ath. pr., C.)
Vārshyāyaṇi, N. Mh. Bh.
† Vālmīki, T.
Vedamitra, Ṛik. pr.
† Vyāḷi, Vyāḍi?, Ṛik. pr., Mh. Bh.
Çatabalāxa, Maudgalya
† Çākaṭāyana, K. Ath. pr. P., Mh. Bh.
Çākapūṇi, N.
Çākala pādakṛit, Ṛik. pr.
Çākalas, Ṛik. pr.
Çākalya, Ṛik. pr. K. P.
Çākalya (sthavira), Ṛik. pr.
Çāṅkhāyana, T.
Çaiṭyāyana, T.
† Çaunaka, K. Ath. pr. P.
Sāṅkṛitya, T.
Saunāgas?, Mh. Bh.
Sthaulashṭhīvin, N.
Sphoṭāyana, P.
Hārīta[1], T.

This list will show that grammatical studies flourished vigorously long before Pāṇini, and the fact is also evident from the many circumstances (incidentally mentioned in the Mahābhāshya) which Profr. Weber has collected[2]. But up to Pāṇini's time the direction these studies followed was limited, and this was caused by the circumstances under which grammatical studies arose—the supposed necessity of preserving the Vedic texts free from change. Thus it was that grammar became a Vedāṅga or a science auxiliary to the one great object of study—the Vedic texts; thus arose in Ancient India the necessity of a complete analysis of the phonetic elements of these texts. That this analysis was carried out with great accuracy of observation is shown by the Prātiçākhyas; they record an immense number of trivial facts and even the most unimportant variations, besides cautions against mispronunciation[3]. These last are of the greatest interest, for they conclusively show that the observations were made long before the authors of the Prātiçākhyas had come into contact with the so-called Dravidian races. Of the errors in pronunciation which arise from this source, and which are perpetuated in many MSS., we do not find here the least trace. Thus it follows that the

1) I have endeavoured to make this list as complete as possible, and have used for this purpose Profr. Max Müller's list (A. S. Lit. as well as Profr. Weber's essay on the Mahābhāshya in Ind. Studien xiii.) and the editions of the Prātiçākhyas already quoted. Ṛik. pr.=Prātiçākhya of the Ṛigveda; T.=Taittirīya prātiçākhya; Ath. pr.=Atharva prātiçākhya; K.=Kātyāyanīya; P.=Pāṇini; N.=Yāska's Nirukta; Mh. Bh.=Mahābhāshya.

2) "Indische Studien" xiii. pp. 403 ffg. Profr. Weber remarks: "Wie sehr denn auch der Verf. des Bhāshya in der Einleitung über den Verfall des grammatischen Studiums zu seiner Zeit klagt, sein Werk selbst, diese reiche darin citirte grammatische Literatur, und manche anekdotenartige Bemerkung darin, legen denn doch für das Gegentheil ein günstiges Zeugniss ab."

3) Ṛik. pr. *a.* xiv.

physiological analysis of sound which is by far the most remarkable feature of the Sanskrit Grammar belongs to the oldest stage of the science.

Of the development of the analysis of words and their forms before Pāṇini, it is also possible to trace something, though not much. For this materials must be sought in the Brāhmaṇas[1]. Some of these I have given already. At the risk of repetition, I shall here sum up the most important inferences. Indian literature of the earliest periods (like is now known to have been the case with nearly all nations) was in verse, and thus matters of prosody occupy the most important part of the discussions in the Brāhmaṇas, with respect to language. But there are indications that more than this was attained at an early period. Etymologies of (for the most part) a very frivolous kind occur in ímmense numbers. These show that doubts and difficulties had already arisen with reference to the ancient rites, and these etymologies are the obvious inventions of theologians who were driven to this resource to support their own views. But this led on to more, and the Brāhmaṇas show already[2] a discrimination between roots[3] and suffixes and grammatical forms. The analysis was, however, not *originally* grammatical. On one side, it was applied to a discussion of the minutest details of the analysis of sound and of the relations of the Pada and Sa*m*hitā texts[4]—hence the Çīxās and Prātiçākhyas. On the other side it was etymological and philosophical—hence the Nirukta and syntactical discussions as regards the meaning of sentences. Of the early treatises that once existed we have unfortunately but few representatives, and these are imperfect[5]; it is, however, not

---

1) It is greatly to be desired, when the Brahmaṇas and other Vedic treatises including the Sūtras may be edited, that some one should give a digest of all the matter they may contribute on such heads as: Geography, Grammar, Prosody, Geometry, etc. In 1869 ("Catalogue", p. 29) I called attention to the importance of parts of the Çrauta sūtras as regards the early history of geometry. Dr. Thibaut (in a very remarkable paper read before the Oriental Congress, 1874) has since worked this out with important results. The other heads are not less worthy of notice; out of the Brāhmaṇas it will be possible to trace the gradual integration of all Indian knowledge. As regards grammar, see above, pp. 26-7.

2) See p. 27 (above) *note* 2.

3) It is perhaps not unnecessary to point out now that, of late, discussions have arisen regarding the value of the root-philology, that the objectionable term 'root' is not Indian. The original word 'dhātu' means 'element'; obviously free from the objections raised to 'root' which is a mistranslation arising out of the philology of the last century.

4) "Nirukta", Naig. i., 17 and Durgācārya's C. on this passage—se 'yā*m* padaprakṛiti*h* sa*m*hitā | sa*m*hitai 'va prakṛiti*h* vikāra*h* padāni." Also Patañjali's "kāni puna*h* çabdānuçāsanasya prayojanāni? raxohāgamalaghvasandehā*h* prayojanam".

5) As seen long ago by Profr. Roth ("Nirukta", p. xx.).

difficult to infer with considerable certainty that they were in verse or çlokas. The oldest parts of the works which represent the primitive Sanskrit Grammar are in verse, and we find mention of very extensive grammatical and other works in çlokas (*e. g.* Vyāḍi's "Saṅgraha") which are anterior to Pāṇini[1]. What relics we still have of the primitive Sanskrit Grammar show that it must have been tolerably complete, and there is sufficient to show that these works did not exactly agree *a*) in technical terms, or *b*) in doctrine, but they agreed generally in their technical system and used mostly words, not symbols. Further inferences would be premature.

Before the time of Pāṇini, Vyākaraṇa was separately recognized as a Vedāṅga, but it is as well to remark that Vyākaraṇa as a science was intended, not any particular author's treatise on the subject. The incompleteness of even the Ṛikprātiçākhya and the fact that it refers to one çākhā only of the Ṛigveda show that it cannot have been the real Vedāṅga-Vyākaraṇa, and Pāṇini's relatively recent date precludes the supposition[2] that his work was the one. That the commentators never intended by Vedāṅga to indicate any single work is shown by such statements as Durgācārya's "Vyākaraṇam ashṭadhā niruktam caturdaçādhā" (on i., 20), and the fact that by Kalpa (also a Vedāṅga) no one ever understood any particular Kalpasūtra out of the many that have existed and still exist[3].

We have seen that the science of grammar existed long before Pāṇini; but if it be taken into consideration that the earliest grammatical treatises must have been handed down orally, and that there is little reason to believe that writing was much used before Pāṇini's time[4], it is difficult to see how these treatises, repeated as school-books, could have escaped

---

1) Goldstücker "Pāṇini's Place", p. 80.

2) Goldstücker ("Pāṇini's Place" pp. 188-218) apparently takes Pāṇini's treatise to be *the* Vedāṅga. See also his remarks in the *Academy* (July, 9. 1870) pp. 270-1.

3) See the excellent remarks of Profr. Roth, "Nirukta", pp. xiv-xxii. and Sāyaṇa's C. on the Ṛigv. i., p. 34 (ed. Max Müller). The only possible way to give an intelligible meaning to the passages which mention the Vedāṅga Vyākaraṇa is to understand them as referring to the science of grammar and not to any special treatise or treatises.

4) See my "Elements of S. Indian Palæography" pp. 3-8. I may here add that writing as practised in India shows that the analysis of Sanskrit phonetics had been carried out by others than those by whom the use of writing was introduced; how otherwise can be explained the absence of a sign for the aspirate, *e. g.* as in kh, gh compared with k and g? Again, it was applied to the Vedas comparatively late; or why should we see y or v (*e. g.*) used to write iy and uv? (cfr. Regnier, "Étude sur l'idiome des Védas" p. 176 etc.)

modification and interpolation. Enough, however, remains to show conclusively that the two most important features of Sanskrit Grammar—the phonetic analysis and the resolution of words into dhātu and pratyaya—belong to its earliest stages and that these discoveries were made spontaneously in India[1].

A question naturally arises here—may not the identification of so many works with the Aindra Grammar, especially as they differ more or less among themselves, be too wide? May not, in short, some of them belong to others of the eight schools? The possibility of error which, of course, exists here seems not to be very material. The enumeration of eight schools of grammar belongs to the 12th century A. D., as has been already mentioned, and we certainly have several of these eight treatises in the condition in which they then were. About Çākaṭāyana's and Jinendra's Grammars there can be no doubt; both differ from the Aindra Grammars and Pāṇini's work in essential points, but they are far nearer to the last. This is also the case with the Candra Grammar which exists in Tibetan, and is known to be a mere improvement on Pāṇini[2]. The treatises of Kāçakṛitsna(-i), Āpiçali and Amara remain, and of these we have no information; but it is difficult to see how any of the treatises I term Aindra, can possibly be by these authors; for nearly all these Aindra treatises profess to be by quite different authors, and there is no valid reason for supposing that these names have been changed: those we actually find attached to them are quite as illustrious as even Kāçakṛitsna, Āpiçali or Amara[3].

It appears to me that this last fact shows conclusively that at the time of the redaction of the Prātiçākhyas to their present form the Vedas had already been reduced to writing; without written Vedas such passages as Ṛik. pr. xvii., 14 are quite unintelligible. The authorities who consider that the Vedas were written at the time the Prātiçākhyas were composed are Roth, Böhtlingk and, of course, Goldstücker. Those who take the opposite view are Weber, Müller, Haug and Westergaard. Much in the Prātiçākhyas is, it appears to me, older than *written* Vedas, much also is later; thus both have reason for their views.

1) It is scarcely necessary to remark that it was Profr. Roth who (in the introduction to his edition of the Nirukta) first pointed out the necessary course of the development of Sanskrit Grammar.

2) Tāranātha, pp. 117 and 152 respectively.

3) The Āpiçali of Pāṇini (vi., 1, 92) was probably a grammarian, but (to judge by a few quotations) the writer of this name referred to by the more recent authors (and Vopadeva?) was a lexicographer. He is quoted by Ujjvaladatta (on Uṇādi s. i., 18 and iv., 174); also by Sāyaṇa (in his Dhātuvṛitti) and in the Padacandrikā (1431 A. D.) as reported by Aufrecht (Z. d. d. M. G. xxviii., p. 111). If Vopadeva's Āpiçali be a lexicographer (as his term 'çābdika' would allow) the Amara he mentions may be the author of the Kosha.

Again it may be said: Çākaṭāyana was one of the oldest of the grammarians, but his technical terms and system entirely disagree with what has been shown above to be characteristic of the Aindra School. This is certainly the case, but I shall show further on[1], that, as we have it, Çākaṭāyana's Grammar is a redaction of the old work done posterior to Pāṇini with a technical system in advance of even Pāṇini. It is for this reason that Vopadeva mentions Çākaṭāyana, for it is evident from the works of the eight grammarians that we still possess, that he mentions them for differences of technical system, and not for differences of doctrine: such differences of doctrine as we find actually recorded, or are possible, are very few and insignificant at the most, and would never have justified a distinction between grammarians who followed the same system of technical terms and arrangement, such as we find Vopadeva actually makes. With the Çākaṭāyana Grammar before us that Vopadeva must have seen, the mention of this work is intelligible. The differences of doctrine (as far as I have been able to find) are very small and few between Pāṇini, Çākaṭāyana and Jinendra; the differences between their technical systems are numerous and important. Lastly it must be remarked that though Vopadeva was well acquainted with the Kātantra[2], he does not mention it, and must, therefore, have included it under one of the eight schools which he knew as predecessors in the science. For these reasons I believe that my conclusions regarding the Aindra Grammar are substantially correct, and that further experience will tend to strengthen them; except, indeed, the general views of the chronology of Sanskrit literature as now received, be somehow entirely upset. But this contingency is barely possible; it is most improbable.

---

1) See Appendix.

2) The reasons for believing that Vopadeva knew of and used the Kātantra are very strong. *a.* He has copied some of the Kātantra terms, *e.g.* li for liṅga as the Commentator (on i., 12) remarks. *b.* The Kāvyakāmadhenu—a commentary on Vopadeva's Kavikalpadruma, and which is attributed by so good an authority as Durgadāsa to Vopadeva himself—quotes Trilocanadāsa's Kātantravṛittipañjikā which was not the first commentary on the Kātantra, and which must, therefore, be long anterior to Vopadeva's date. (Cfr. on this point Aufrecht's "Catalogus" pp. 170 and 175). Besides, *c.* Ujjvaladatta (13th century) quotes the Kātantra though he did not know apparently of Vopadeva who lived a little before him. So Maitreya Raxita (the oldest writer on dhātus, cfr. Westergaard's "Radices" p. ii.) also quotes the Kālāpa (or Kātantra) Grammar.

III.

It is now necessary to consider if it be possible to trace in any way the innovations Pāṇini made in the treatment of Sanskrit Grammar; it appears to me that this can be done successfully to a very considerable extent, though a difference of opinion must always exist as to a few details.

There can be no question that Pāṇini's Grammar made an epoch in Indian literature; his name occurs everywhere, his treatise soon superseded all others, and has exercised the ingenuity of a countless number of followers. Certainly, for near two thousand years, Pāṇini's word has been law in India on all questions of grammar. It is evident that for it to have gained such a position of authority in so conservative a country as India, it must have been vastly superior in the eyes of the Brahmans to all the numerous treatises which must have been in existence before Pāṇini's time: the Tibetan writers[1] (whatever may have been their authority for saying so) cannot be far wrong in making out that Pāṇini's work was the first complete and systematic treatise on Grammar. It is also tolerably plain that the circumstances under which this book was composed differed greatly from the older stage of Indian history; without some contact with foreign peoples and bitter disputes among religious sects at home, such highly developed enquiry into language as Pāṇini's treatise displays, is contrary to all experience. Until Greeks began to teach their language to the Romans, grammar made but little progress[2], and the origin of Arabic and Hebrew Grammar is due to the contact of the Semitic races of Arabia with Persians, Syrians and other foreigners. The latest and most probable conclusions as to the date of Pāṇini point to such a period in Indian events, when Buddhism had become a prominent, if not the most prominent, religion in Northern India, and an intercourse with the Persians and Greeks had begun which soon became of vast importance owing to the long continuance of the Bactrian kingdom. The influence of Buddhism on grammatical studies has been lately pointed out by Mr. Sayce; he says[3]: "it is very possible that the Sanskrit grammarians were excited to their work by the native dialects, which had been quickened into activity and raised to the level of respectability by the spread of

---

1) Tāranātha (by Schiefner) pp. 48 and 54 respectively.

2) Teuffel, "Geschichte der Römischen Literatur", § 50.

3) "Principles of Comparative Philology", p. 246.

Buddhism." This remark is, I believe, new, but it is perfectly just. Observations of dialectic variations of pronunciation and of forms of words occur very early in the Sanskrit grammatical literature, and if they are not to be found in Pāṇini's Grammar it is evident that the system of the work precludes insertion of such matter. There are several notices of provincialisms in the Mahābhāshya which have been collected by Profr. Weber[1], and the Mīmā*m*sā sūtras attributed to Jaimini also shew that foreign or local words were early noticed even in the Vedas[2]. Pāṇini's sūtras mention several foreign kingdoms, though it is not, perhaps, altogether safe to assume that some are not interpolations. Thus circumstances would lead, at the period when Pāṇini lived, to a far more comprehensive and philosophical study of language than had as yet obtained, remarkable in every way though the results already arrived at were; and, as there is much reason to believe that Sanskrit was, at that time, rapidly becoming extinct, this must also have led to increased zeal in observing and classifying facts. The history of grammatical studies in many other countries points irresistably to this conclusion.

Pāṇini's innovations come (as far as I have been able to trace them) under four heads: (1) the invention of the Çivasūtras and of the use of pratyāhāras for groups of terminations; also the extensive use of gaṇas, if not their invention; (2) the invention of a new system of anubandhas; (3) the invention or more exact use of several technical terms; (4) the use of a technical syntax and a more elaborate system of sūtras.

1. The entire absence of the Çivasūtras as part of the technical system of the Aindra treatises has been already repeatedly noticed[3], as also the absence of such pratyāhāras as tiṅ, sup, taṅ[4] which are formed on the same principle, *i.e.*, by giving the first and last letter of a series of letters or terms. I may add here that the Sanskrit grammarians have always regarded the Çivasūtras as the essence or revealed part of his grammar. Thus Nāgoji says: "teshā*m* anāditvād eshā*m* Pāṇinikṛi-

---

1) "Indische Studien", xiii., pp. 365-6.

2) See Jaimini-s i., 3, 10 and Kumārila Bhaṭṭa's C. on this passage. The çīxās notice some such details (Haug, "Ved. Accent", p. 64).

For the Indian philological views regarding foreign languages see my "Elements of S. Indian Palæography" p. 85. In this respect the Indian grammarians were, perhaps, weakest. See Profr. Max Müller's A. S. L. (2nd. ed.) pp. 117-8 on the early observation of dialectical and other peculiarities; also his note in Z. d. d. M. G. Vol. vii. on the same subject.

3) pp. 23, 24, 29.

4) pp. 29-30.

tatvāt"—for those (Çivasūtras) are without origin, these (the rest of the grammar) were composed by Pāṇini. So the original edition of Pāṇini[1] edited under Colebrooke's superintendence begins with the verse:

Yenā 'xarasamāmnāyam adhigamya Maheçvarāt |
Kṛitsna*m* vyākaraṇa*m* prokta*m* tasmai Pāṇinaye nama*h* ||

This is from the Pāṇinīya-çixā (Yajurv. recension, edited by Weber, p. 359), and, therefore, is probably of a very respectable age. But I think that Pāṇini's authorship is also proved by his explanation of the use of these sūtras (i., 1, 71)—"ādir antyena sahe 'tā". If he were not the first to use these sūtras, his explanation, as here given, is superfluous and contrary to his own expressed intention.

I have remarked above on the use of gaṇas in the various grammatical treatises which I have compared.

2. The invention of a new system of anubandhas. This is stated by Patañjali in a passage which was first pointed out by the late Profr. Goldstücker[2]. This passage is as follows; it occurs in the discussion on the sūtra vii., 1, 18 ("auṅa āpa*h*")—"athavā pūrvasūtranirdeço 'yam | pūrvasūtreshu ca ye 'nubandhā na tair ihe 'tkāryāṇi kriyante"[3]. Patañjali here states that there were grammatical sūtras by predecessors of Pāṇini in which anubandhas were used, but that they had no effect in Pāṇini's treatise. This statement is of great value, for it settles a question which would be otherwise left undetermined by the existing Aindra treatises. Anubandhas do not occur in the Tolkāppiyam: indeed, it is impossible to see what use they could be in a grammar of one of the so-called Dravidian languages. Nor is there any place for them in the Prātiçākhyas. It would be useless to consider the Kātantra and Kaccāyana's Grammar which furnish a few, as these do not throw any light on the subject; the latter treatise expressly states that "technical terms (used) by other (grammarians) are used (here)"[4]. It would thus be very hazardous to draw any inferences from a comparison of these with the anubandhas used by Pāṇini, for we have not a standard such as the Tolkāppiyam furnishes in respect of the technical terms, and the few that occur in the Kātantra are again different. The differences between Sanskrit

1) Calcutta, Ç. 1731. p. 1.

2) "Pāṇini's Place", p. 181 (Sep. imp.).

3) Benares ed. f. 57.

4) ed. Senart, p. 10 (sūtra. i., 1, 9). The sūtra appears to include anubandhas as well as technical terms such as are mentioned by the commentary.

and Pali would naturally lead to a difference of treatment in this respect; nor is there any reason to believe that the old grammarians who preceded Pāṇini were more uniform in respect of the anubandhas they used than in their use of technical terms. The fact remains that Pāṇini invented a new system, and it is obvious that the principle on which he selected the letters he uses as prefixes and suffixes, was the avoidance, if possible, of unnecessary confusion; he has not, however, always succeeded, but his display of ingenuity is very remarkable.

3. The invention or more exact use of several technical terms.

The technical terms used by Pāṇini are of two kinds: *a*) a word used as a type of a class; or *b*) a purely conventional symbol (kṛitrimā*h* sa*m*jñā*h* as Patañjali calls them).

Of the first (*a*) class the following are examples:—kṛit, as a name of the affixes by which primary nouns are formed; nadī, a name for certain feminine nouns in -ī and -ū; strī, as a name of feminine nouns; gotra, as a general name for descendants of a man; saṅkhyā, as a name of numerals. The origin of these is evident; except the two last mentioned, they appear to be the first words of original gaṇas. Such terms we find in the Kātantra[1] and it is probable that they formed part of the older treatises.

The terms of the second class are remarkable; examples in Pāṇini are—gha (= -tara and -tama); ghi (= -i and -u); ghu (= √da, √dhā, etc.); ṭi (=the last vowel in a word and following consonant or consonants); bha used as a name of what Bopp termed the weakest cases; it—as a name of anubandhas.

Of these ghu, ṭi and bha are certainly older than Pāṇini, if we are to believe Patañjali, as the late Profr. Goldstücker pointed out. Similar symbols occur in the Kātantra[2] and still more in Kaccāyana's grammar[3] though (as might be expected) not identical with Pāṇini's. These symbols must, therefore, have been used in the older treatises. Here again we have no standard of comparison, for such terms are wanting in the Tolkāppiyam, but it seems likely that there were many such symbols in use, for we find others in the Vājasaneya Prātiçākhya[4]. Pāṇini probably made a selection, and used those more accurately (as Goldstücker sug-

1) *e. g.* Agni (ii., 1, 8); nadī (ii., 1, 9 etc.); çraddhā (ii., 1, 10), etc.

2) *e. g.* Ghuṭ (ii., 1, 3. for the sarvanāmasthāna cases); dhuṭ (ii., 1, 18); nu (ii., 2, 11) etc.

3) Ga, a name of the vocative (ii., 1, 6); gha, final ā (ii., 1, 9); jha (ii., 1, 7); pa (ii., 1, 8); la, etc.

4) *e. g.* sim, jit, mud, dhi as names of classes of letters.

gested); others, again, such as çlu, luk, etc. are probably his own invention. It would be interesting to discuss all the symbols we find used in the earlier and later grammatical treatises, but this laborious task would only show the growth of method in Sanskrit Grammar, and would throw no light on the point to which I have devoted this monograph.

The origin of these symbols is an interesting question, but involved in much obscurity. Some are, no doubt, merely arbitrary symbols, but others are, it is certain, the abbreviations of real words. Thus Dr. Bühler has suggested that 'it' is for 'iti', a derivation that at once commends itself. It is certain that the symbols used in the Phulla (resp. Pushpa) sūtras (which teach the formation of the Sāma verses as recited) are merely mutilated words; thus, *e. g.* bha is for sto-bha; tara for rathan-tara; hārādi for prati-hārādi[1].

Thus, in respect of symbolic and other technical terms, the only possible conclusion is, that Pāṇini used some of those invented by his predecessors, made them more precise, and added new terms of his own. He extended this system, originally only applied to details, to the entire grammar; his system banishes all traces of the philosophical analysis of the language, and presents a purely conventional representation in which phonetics and etymology, originally kept separate, are completely fused.

4. The use of a more elaborate and technical syntax and a more elaborate system of sūtras.

Here it is possible to arrive at a more exact conclusion as to what innovations Pāṇini made[2]. It has been well remarked by Regnier that the tendency in the Sanskrit style of composition is to exaggerate synthesis[3], and this peculiarity is carried to excess in the sūtras of Pāṇini

---

1) As was first pointed out by Profr. Weber, "Ind. Studien" i., p. 46.

2) Profr. Max Müller has distinguished the several styles of composition which can be found in the earlier Sanskrit (Vedic) works, in his "Ancient Sanskrit Literature".

3) "Étude sur l' idiome des Védas" (1855) p. vii. As this book is not common I shall give a few of M. Regnier's excellent remarks: "Cette gradation toujours croissante de la synthèse finit par aboutir à un dernier degré, qui est vraiment, ce semble, la dernière et infranchissable limite de la puissance de combinaison au moyen du discours. Je me hâte de dire, et on le comprend avant que je le dise, que ce dernier excès appartient à une manière de langage tout artificielle. L'ultrasynthétisme peut être naturel et populaire; les idiomes de certains peuples sauvages nous en donnent la preuve; mais, dans ces idiomes, cette fusion, qu'on peut appeler confusion, tient à ce qu'ils ne savent pas décomposer, discerner les éléments de la pensée; tandis que, dans l'excès de combinaison dont je parle, c'est avec des matériaux bien distincts, des mots que la grammaire et le lexique présentent comme autant d'unités separées,

who has not only exhausted the natural resources of the copious system of inflections presented by Sanskrit, but has added new and peculiar meanings to some of the cases—such as the ablative and locative[1], and with him even the arrangement of words is full of meaning[2]. But there is nothing of this in the works that I have classed together as belonging to the Aindra School, which are all written in a concise but hardly technical style; the sūtras are aphorisms and are sometimes obscure, but they are not algebraical formulas like the sūtras of Pāṇini. Again in the sūtras of Pāṇini we find a syntactical concatenation which is almost wanting in the older sūtras, *e. g.* a sūtra is often of a word or words in the genitive case, but this is required by a nominative in a sūtra, often far before it.

It is hardly necessary to remark that the sūtra style was in use before Pāṇini and that Patañjali mentions grammatical sūtras anterior to him, but he refined on this style of composition to a great extent. Thus (as grammarians tell us) he omitted the paribhāshās[3] or rules respecting the logical method of his treatise, and which always form a part of Indian scientific treatises. The almost incredible complications of the Pāṇinīya paribhāshās are now—thanks to Profr. Kielhorn—no longer an insuperable difficulty to students. These sūtras chiefly determine conflicts of rules and similar matters, and present the greatest contrast to the simple method of the older treatises which have only the simple artifice of division into adhikaraṇas or topics.

This very brief survey of Pāṇini's technical system enables us to add a few new details in regard to the system of his predecessors, which cannot be gathered from the existing treatises that represent now the earlier

---

qu'on parvient à former sciemment et à dessein cette chaîne de ténèbres dont parle, dans un autre sens, le livre de la Sagesse, *catena tenebrarum*, et à enfermer la pensée dans les liens d'une longue nuit, *vinculis longae noctis compedire* (ch. xvii., v. 2 et 17), ou des esprits européens, habitués à la forme de la pensée moderne, ont souvent bien de la peine à porter la lumière et à trouver leur voie. J'ai dit qu'une telle manière d'écrire ne pouvait être qu'artificielle, et elle l'est en effect. C'est dans la prose philosophique et technique que nous la rencontrons. Je ne veux pas parler de l'algèbre des grammairiens, des formules de Pāṇini: il y a dans la construction de ces axiomes une grande puissance d'esprit, et la langue y montre une incroyable aptitude à la concision; mais ce n'est point là du style, c'est comme je le disais, de l'algèbre. La forme de discours et de construction que j'ai en vue ici, je la trouve dans l'exposition et dans la dialectique des grammairiens, des interprètes."

1) "Tasmād ity uttarasya" i., 1, 67; "tasminn iti nirdishṭe pūrvasya" i., 1, 66.

2) *e. g.* "Sthāne 'ntaratamaḥ" i., 1, 50; "yathāsaṅkhyam anudeçaḥ samānām" i., 3, 10.

3) Profr. Kielhorn's "Paribhāshenduçekhara" p. i.

stages of Sanskrit Grammar, but which do not contradict the results arrived at by an examination of those works. So far, then, the results at which I have arrived are confirmed from this point of view.

It has long been recognized that Pāṇini's date is of the utmost importance in Indian literary history, and it has been discussed with great care[1]. The result, as now accepted, is that he lived in the 4th century B. C.; I cannot see that there is any reason why he should not be placed nearly a century later, which would remove some difficulties that the earlier date presents. But, though his name will always be great, we do know but little about him, and there is no probability that we shall ever know more. That he was born at Çālātura in the extreme north-west of India is certain; his mother's name was Dāxī[2], or perhaps this only indicates her race[3]. His life was probably uneventful, though tradition says that he met with a violent death, being killed by a lion[4].

Whatever merits may be fairly attributed to his predecessors, it cannot be disputed that Pāṇini's work was stupendous in respect of Sanskrit, and he made a good beginning of a grammar of the Vedic language. For two thousand years no one in India has been able to do better. It is thus no matter for surprise that his life should be the subject to which (like that of his still greater countryman Buddha)[5] the common-places of mythology have attached themselves. In the story of the idle stupid boy who suddenly became the greatest scholar that India ever saw, one can recognize the "Boots" or "Aschenputtel" of our nursery tales[6]—he sits idle and despised at home, till the time comes for his real nature to show itself. That he got supernatural assistance is also in accordance with the same old stories, and in this particular case is entirely in unison with the Buddhist and Vedantist notions; that Çiva gave this aid, seems to have arisen out of the popular name for the first 14 sūtras being

1) The latest are Profr. Goldstücker's "Pāṇini's Place", and Profr. Weber's strictures on it in Vol. V. of his "Indische Studien", pp. 1-176 (1862).

2) Patañjali on vii., 1, 18.

3) The "Saṃyaminămamālikā" by a Çaṅkara (Tanjore MS. No. 10. 463) has (çl. 5-6). . . . . Granthakartā ca sūtrakṛit (5) Çālāturīyako Dāxīputraḥ Pāṇinir Āhikaḥ |

4) Pañcatantra ed. Kosegarten ii., 34 (= ii., 32 of the Bombay edition, but not in the oldest recension): Siṃho vyākaraṇasya kartur aharat prāṇān priyān Pāṇineḥ.

5) See Senart's "Essai sur la légende du Buddha" in the "*Journal Asiatique*" vii. ième série, t. ii., pp. 118 ffg.

6) Grimm "Kinder- und Hausmährchen", iii., pp. 37-9. Dasent "Tales from the Norse" *passim* cfr. also the Psalm cli. (in some old rituals): "Pusillus eram inter fratres meos, et adolescentior in domo patris mei" etc. (of David) — "Ps. Mozarabicum" (*ed.* 1775) lxv., *a*.

misunderstood. The only fact in the legend is that Pāṇini's grammar superseded those of his predecessors; and these, with reference to the Vedic legend already[1] given, became an 'Indra Grammar'. The reason why this name was given to treatises by his predecessors is not far to seek. Like all Indian sciences, grammar began out of a study of the texts used for sacrificial purposes, and when by imperceptible degrees it became a rudimentary science, a divine origin was, as a matter of course, attributed to it. Taught orally and writing being almost unknown, the primitive systems could not preserve enough individuality to bear the names of their authors, and were in the same position as the Brāhmaṇas. When writing became more general, Pāṇini's genius could thus render his name lasting; the names of most of his predecessors could only be recollected in connection with details in which they differed, or by their discoveries.

IV.

I shall now try to enumerate the different treatises in Sanskrit and other languages which appear to attach themselves to the Aindra or older Grammar. I shall do so briefly, as several of the most important are known by editions that have nothing remaining to be said, and others in MSS. are as yet beyond my reach or are of comparatively little value. We may reasonably expect to see in a few years more, sufficient descriptions of the Sanskrit and Pali MSS. known at present by name only, and then I may hope to be able to continue what I have here begun, and to attempt to show the historical development of the Aindra as opposed to the Pāṇinīya grammar. To begin with the Phonetic treatises—

I. SANSKRIT.
a. Çixās.

first in **Sanskrit** we have the tracts called Çixā, most of which have been only recently discovered. Those actually known are mentioned in ordinary type; those only known by quotation are in spaced type.

1. Amoghanandinī çixā[2]
Āraṇyakaçixā[3]
C.

Kātyāyanaçixā[4]
K ā h a l a ç i x ā[5]
5. Keçavī çixā[6]

---

1) p. 6, *note* 4.
2) Rājendralāl Mitra, "Notices" i., p. 72.
3) Mysore Cat. No. 51.
4) Rājendralāl Mitra, "Report", p. 18.
5) Mentioned in the C. on the Siddhāntaçixā.
6) Rājendralāl Mitra, "Report", p. 18.

Kauçikī çīxā[1]
Gautamī çīxā[2]
Taittirīyaçīxā (?)[3]
Nāradaçīxā[4]
C. (Nāradīyaçīxāvivaraṇa) by Çobhākara[5]
10. Pāṇinīyaçīxā, two recensions[6]
a. Ṛigveda
b. Yajurveda
CC. by Çesha and another[7] there is also a
C. by Sāyaṇa ('Çīxābhāshya')[8]
C. (Svaravigraha)[9]
Pārāçaraçīxā[10]
Bodhāyanaçīxā[11]
Bhāradvājaçīxā[12]
— Vyākhyāna[13]
Māṇḍūkī çīxā[14]
15. Lomaçanyaçīxā[15] or Lomeçiç. (by Garga)
Vālmīkiçīxa[16]
Vaçishṭaçīxā[17]
Vyāsaçīxā[18]
Vyākhyāna by Svarāvadhānin[19]
Çambhuçīxā[20]
20. Çīxādicatushṭaya (?)[21]
Çīxāsamuccaya[22]
Sarvasammataçīxā[23]
— Commentary[24]
Siddhāntaçīxā by Çrīnivāsin
— Vyākhyāna[25]
24. Hāritaçīxā[26]

---

1) "Notices," i., p. 72.

2) Haug, "Ueber das Wesen" u. s. w. p. 61, *n.* 1. This exists in the Tamiḷ country.

3) Whitney, "Taitt. Prātiç." p. 435 (cfr. xx., 12). See also extracts from a similar work quoted in the C. of the Ath. pr. (ed. Whitney, p. 261).

4) See my "Catalogue" p. 42. Haug *u. s.* p. 55, *n.* 1 "Notices", i., p. 73. Profr. Haug's remarks render it probable that two recensions exist.

5) "Notices", i., p. 73.

6) Both edited by Profr. Weber—"Indische Studien" iv., pp. 345-371.

7) Gujarat Catalogue (by Bühler), i., p. 206 (No. 56) and p. 210 (No. 75).

8) N. W. Prov. Catalogue, pp. 14 and 34 (Nos. 46 and 102).

9) Oudh Catalogue, iv., p. 6.

10) "Report", p. 18.

11) Mentioned in C. on Siddhānta çīxā. See my Catalogue, p. 9.

12) My Catalogue, p. 8. Guj. Cat. i., p. 206 (No. 60).

13) Mysore Catalogue, No. 51.

14) Haug, *u. s.* p. 55. Weber, "Pratijñāsūtra" pp. 106 ffg. "Notices" i., p. 73.

15) "Report", p. 18. Haug, *u. s.* p. 61. "Notices", i., p. 71.

16) Mentioned in the C. on the Siddhāntaç. and by Ahobala Bhaṭṭa in his C. on the Āndhraçabdacintāmaṇi.

17) Mentioned in the C. on the Siddhāntaç. Mysore Cat. No. 51.

18) Mysore Cat. No. 52. Mentioned by Ahobala Bhaṭṭa.

19) Mysore No. 52.

20) Mentioned in the C. on the Siddhāntaçīxā.

21) Gujarat Cat. i., p. 210 (No. 74). Probably Çīxā, Jyotisha, Chandas and Nirukta.

22) Mysore Cat. No. 57.

23) Do. do. do.

24) My Catalogue, p. 8. Mysore Cat. No. 51.

25) Do. p. 9. do. do.

26) Mentioned in the C. on the Siddhāntaçīxā. See my "Catalogue", p. 9.

Of these the first, fifth, twenty-first and twenty-third are most probably modern compilations; several others (Gautamī, Nārada, Maṇḍūkī and Lomaçanya) refer to the Sāmaveda, and it is thus difficult to compare them with other grammatical works, for reasons I have already given; the age of the remaining ones is not yet positively determined, and before this can be attempted in a satisfactory manner, critical editions must be published[1]. Dr. Haug[2] is inclined apparently to think that they represent an earlier stage than the Prātiçākhyas, and distinguishes the two classes of works very aptly. He says[3]: "Was nun den Inhalt der Çīxās und Prātiçākhyas betrifft, so ist er nicht identisch, wenn sie auch Vieles gemeinsam haben, da der Zweck für welche beide Arten von Werken verfasst sind, ein Verschiedener ist. Die Çīxās lehren nur die Aussprache und Recitation der wedischen Texte im Allgemeinen, und beziehen sich auf keine bestimmte Form derselben; die Prātiçākyas dagegen setzen immer einen Pada-Text voraus, und lehren, wie aus demselben eine Sa*m*hitā zu construiren ist. ....In den çīxās dagegen sind alle Differenzen des Sa*m*hitā-Textes von dem des Pada ausgelassen; ebenso fehlen alle Andeutungen über den Krama. Das chronologische Verhältniss der çīxās zu den Prātiçākhyas anlangend, so halte ich die ersteren für entschieden älter als die letztere. Die erstern waren vorhanden, ehe sich das Bedürfniss nach den letztern regte. Die Prātiçākhyas setzen bereits eingehende grammatische Studien voraus, während für die çīxās ein geringeres Mass derselben verlangt wird. Zudem können die Prātiçākhyas nur zu einer Zeit entstanden sein, als man anfing, den Wedatext in die verschiedensten Formen zu bringen, um ihn desto unverfälschter überliefern zu können. Diess war ohne Zweifel ein langer Process, der solche Elementarkenntnisse in der Phonetik voraussetzt, wie wir sie in den çīxās finden. Die Prātiçākhyas, die nach einem umfassenderen Plane, als die çixās angelegt waren, nahmen nicht nur (64) die Lehren dieser in sich auf, sondern führten sie auch weiter." It would be difficult to explain the existence of the çīxās on other grounds than those here stated, and it is obvious that these Tracts, though perhaps owing their present forms to relatively late reductions, preserve much that is really primitive. Profr. Weber has lately pointed out one verse in the Pāṇinīyaçīxā (R. 52), which is quoted by Patañjali[4].

---

1) I believe that we may soon hope to see two or three edited by Profr. Kielhorn.

2) *u. s.* p. 53 ffg.

3) Do. p. 63-4.

4) "Indische Studien", xiii., p. 399.

The term Pāṇinīya as applied to this çixā would merely show that it was popular after Pāṇini's time; for it is very common to find that in India substantially old works have modern claptrap names assigned to them[1]. But there is much in it actually copied from Pāṇini. Thus we find occasionaly pratyāhāras, *e.g.* 'eṅ', though the old system is also followed (çl. 29 etc.). Pāṇini is also mentioned by name as Dāxīputra. Other verses are probably primitive.

To this class of works (but to a very limited extent) the Pushpa (or rather Phulla) sūtra belongs; it teaches how to form the gaṇas of the Sāmaveda, and so far as the discussion of the phonetic elements goes, it uses the old terms and not pratyāhāras.

5. Prātiçākhyas. The next important class of phonetic treatises that can be connected with the Aindra School of grammar includes the Prātiçākhyas; all of these that have been discovered have been edited in an incomparable manner. They are as follows:

1. **Rigvedaprâtiçâkhya** (attributed to Çaunaka), edited and translated (in German and French) by Profr. Max Müller and Mons. A. Regnier[2].

On this there are two commentaries; the oldest is a vṛitti discovered by Profr. Eggeling in a Grantha MS., and described by him in the preface to Profr. Max Müller's edition. The best known commentary is the 'Pārshadavyākhyā' by Ūvaṭa Bhaṭṭa, son of Vajraṭa, an inhabitant of Ānandapura (? Benares). This was first brought into notice by Profr. Roth[3], and exists in many MSS. Copious extracts from it are given by Mons. Regnier. The introduction (from Tanjore MS. No. 2417) is as follows:

Sūtrabhāshyakṛita*h* sarvān praṇamya çirasā çuci*h* |
Çaunaka*m* ca viçesheṇa yene 'da*m* pārshada*m* kṛitam ||
Tathā vṛittikṛita*h* sarvā*m*s tān sūtrayaçasas tathā |
Teshā*m* prasādād eteshā*m* svaçaktyā vṛittim ārabhe ||
Lekhyadoshanivṛittyartha*m* vistarārtha*m* kvacit kvacit |
Jñānārtha*m* paṭhanārtha*m* ca yojyate sā mayā puna*h* ||
Tasyā*h* sāmāpane çakti*m* ta eva pradiçantu me |
Labdhvā kāmam aha*m* tebhya*h* prameya*m* pāram īpsitam ||
Ca*m*pāyā*m* nyavasat pūrva*m* Vatsānā*m* kulam ṛiddhimat |
Yasmin dvijavarā jātā bahvṛicā*h* pāragottamā*h* ||

---

1) Thus Dr. Bühler has ascertained that the Vishṇu Smṛiti is really the Kāṭhaka Dharma (Z. d. D. M. G.) xxii., p. 327.

2) 1856-1859 and 1857-1869.

3) "Zur Literatur und Geschichte des Weda", 1846. The introduction is also given there.

Devamitra iti khyātas tasmiṅ jāto mahāmatiḥ |
Sa cai 'sha pārshadaçreshṭhaḥ sutas tasya mahātmanaḥ ||
Nāmnā tu Vishṇumitraḥ sa kumāra iti çasyate |
Tene 'yam yojitā vṛittiḥ samxiptā pārshade sphuṭā ||
Parigṛihṇantu viprendrāḥ suprasannā imām mama |
Ajñānād yad ayuktam syāt tad ṛijūkṛitya gṛihyatām ||
Çāstrāvatāram sambandham shaḍvidham parikīrtayan |
Jñātvā grāhyam bhavec chāstrāvatāram ucyate ||
Atha—Çaunako gṛihapatir vai naimishīyais tu samsthitaiḥ |
Dīxāsu coditaḥ prāha sattre tu dvādaçāhike || iti
Çāstrāvatāram smaranti etc.

2. **Taittirîyaprâtiçâkhya** of the Black Yajurveda.

This, together with its commentary ("Tribhāshyaratna"), has been edited and translated by Profr. Whitney[1]. The author of the commentary is not known; he professes to follow Vararuci, Ātreya and Māhisheya who had composed commentaries on this treatise but which are now apparently lost[2]. It cannot be of any considerable antiquity as it refers to a 'Kālanirṇaya'[3] which is probably the work by Sāyaṇa (14th century).

3. **Vâjasaneyi** or **Kâtyâyana-Prâtiçâkhya** of the White Yajurveda.

This has been edited with extracts from Ūvaṭa's C., and translated (into German) by Profr. Weber[4].

Another Commentary ("Prātiçākhyajyotsnā") is quite recent viz., of the end of the last or beginning of this century; it is by one Rāmacandra son of Siddheçvara. A section of it has been published by Thibaut[5].

4. **Çaunakîya-Câturâdhyâyikâ**, which Profr. Whitney has edited and translated into English[6]. He has demonstrated that it belongs to the Atharvaveda. There is an anonymous commentary which Profr. Whitney has used[7].

A Prātiçākhya of the Sāmaveda is alluded to by Nāgoji Bhaṭṭa[8], but it is not quite clear what he intends, and a work of this name has

1) 1871 (New Haven).
2) pp. 6-7 and 434-5.
3) p. 435.
4) "Indische Studien", iv., pp. 65-160 and 177-331 (1858).
5) "Das Jaṭāpaṭala" (1870), pp. 36-53.
6) 1862 (New Haven).
7) See Profr. Weber's "Verzeichniss" p. 87 (No. 361).
8) Goldstücker in the '*Academy*', 9th July 1870 p. 275: "Sāmalaxaṇam prātiçākhyam çāstram." Several existing books partly answer to this description, *e.g.* the Ṛiktantra and Sāmatantra.

not, as yet, been discovered. It is also likely that some other works of the same nature may yet be in existence. Dr. Haug remarks[1]: "Ich zweifle nicht, dass noch weitere Prātiçākhyas aufgefunden werden; so vermisse ich bis jetzt das zu der Maitrāyaṇī-Saṃhitā, die so vieles Eigenthümliche hat, und gewiss ein besonderes Prātiçākhya besitzt". Theoretically the number of these works should correspond with the number of the Vedic çākhās, but it may be reasonably doubted if this ever was the case.

c. Etymological and general treatises on Grammar.

The Çīxās and Prātiçākhyas represent, so far, one side of the oldest form of the Aindra Grammar—the phonetic analysis of the language; the other side—etymology, is of equal interest, but unfortunately there is little left to represent the older system in this respect. The numerous passages in the Brāhmaṇas have already been mentioned[2], but apart from these we have only one Nirukta (out of 14 that once existed) viz.,

I. **Yâska's Nirukta,** a treatise well-known by Profr. Roth's edition[3], and which, though it exists in two recensions[4], is, no doubt, preserved nearly in its original condition. Yāska gives a general view of the etymological principles known in his time[5], but the arrangement of the book is not grammatical, and to exhibit his system of analysis of words and grammatical forms would require too much space to be possible here; it generally agrees with the so-called Aindra treatises[6]. It must be remarked that there were two schools of etymologists—those headed by Çākaṭāyana who asserted that every noun was derived from a dhātu, and others headed by Gārgya who only gave a partial assent to this theory. Yāska's treatise was not neglected by commentators of whom the earliest appears to have been

a. Skandasvāmin. The commentary (ṭīkā) by this writer is often quoted[7], but is not as yet known to scholars, though it appears to be in existence[8].

1) *u. s.* p. 68.

2) pp. 26 ffg.

3) 8° Göttingen, 1852.

4) *ed.* Roth p. iv.

5) *ed.* Roth p. 31, translated by Profr. Max Müller, in his A. S. L. pp. 164 ffg.

6) See above, p. 12.

7) By Durgācārya and Sāyaṇa in his C. on the Ṛigveda.

8) Central Prov. Cat. p. 8, No. 89—"Niruktaṭīkā", 86 *ll.* 1200 çlokas. (? Incomplete) Durgācārya also calls it Niruktaṭīkā.

b. Durgâcârya wrote a copious commentary—the Niruktavṛitti; this is well known and exists in several MSS. The author seems to have been a native of S. India, and probably lived in the 15th or 16th century A. D. His introduction is one of the most interesting parts of his book, as he there gives an account of his authorities and method; I have already printed it in the introduction to my edition of the Va*m*çabrāhmaṇa[1].

No general treatise on grammar of a date previous to Pāṇini appears to be now extant in its original condition, though there must have been several such, and some at least appear to have been preserved down to Kaiyaṭa's time. Thus he mentions Kuṇi as a predecessor of Pāṇini, but this name does not occur in the older books. Again the Saunāgas, Kuṇara Vaḍava and Vaḍava are also mentioned by the commentators as well as a work, the 'Bhrāja-Çlokas' by Kātyāyana, which was probably an Aindra treatise. Lastly, the Saṅgraha of Vyāḷi may also have belonged to the same school.

There are some smaller tracts which, though since modified, apparently took their origin from the Aindra School. Such are

II. 1. **Çântanava's "Phiṭsûtras."**

2. **Jaṭâpaṭala,** attributed in S. India to Vyāḍi.

These (and, perhaps, some others) just retain sufficient of the old terms to show their origin, but it is evident that they have been repeatedly altered.

d. Kātantra and systems of Grammar derived from it.

The next work of this school in chronological position, and, therefore, in importance, is the Kātantra. Around this, besides commentaries, it will be convenient to group some other allied books.

I. **Kâtantra** or **Kâlâpa-Vyâkaraṇa.** This is now well-known by Profr. Eggeling's excellent edition begun in the Bibl. Indica. The author's name is commonly given as Sarvavarman[2].

Commentaries on it are:

a. Kātantravṛitti by Durgasi*m*ha, edited by Profr. Eggeling in his edition of the text. On this there is more than one commentary. The author wrote a 'ṭīkā' on his own Vṛitti, and again a series of notes—'Candrikā'. There are also notes on Durgasi*m*ha's Vyākhyā (? vṛitti) by Caṅga Dāsa[3].

1) Preface pp. xxxi-xxxiii.

2) The Tibetans, however, say Saptavarman. Colebrooke ("Essays" ii., p. 44) says: "The rules or aphorisms are ascribed to the God Kumāra. It is much used in Bengal."

3) Oudh Cat. vi., p. 6.

aa. Kātantravṛittipañjikā, by Trilocanadāsa[1].

aaa. A gloss on the last, by Suseṇācārya[2].

b. Kātantralaghuvṛitti, by Bhāvasena.

This is a Jain treatise which I found in 1872 in the province of S. Canara. It follows the C. of Durgasiṁha (which it quotes) very closely, and begins:

Sarvajñaṁ sarvavāgīçaṁ bhuktimuktipradāyakam |
Natvā Kātantrasūtrāṇāṁ laghuvṛittir vidhāsyate ||
Yathā bālaprabodhaḥ syāt tathai 've 'daṁ nirūpyate |
Xamadhvaṁ sarvavidvāṁso laxaṇādinirūpaṇe. ||

"Siddho varṇasamāmnāyaḥ" || 1 || varṇānāṁ samāmnāyaḥ pāṭhakramaḥ sakalalokaprasiddho veditavyaḥ etc.

c. Kātantravṛitti by Çrīpati[3]. This same author also wrote a pariçishṭa or supplement to the text[4], which has been commented on more than once:

cc. Pariçishṭaprabodha, by Gopīnātha[5].

ccc. Pariçishṭasiddhāntaratnākara, by Çivarāmacakravartin[6].

d. Kātantravistara, by Vardhamāna[7].

e. Kalāpatattvārṇava, by Raghunandana[8].

f. 'Caitrukuṭī, a C., by a Vararuci[9].

g. Vyākhyāsāra, by Harirāma Cakravartin[10].

h. Do. by Rāmadāsa[11].

Colebrooke[12] mentions also commentaries by:

j. Rāmanātha, [Kātantravṛittiprabodha (in "Notices" iii., p. 83) and said to be a gloss on Rāma's C.]

k. Umāpati

l. Kulacandra

1) See Weber's "Verzeichniss" p. 220 (No. 777), Aufrecht's "Catalogus", p. 169, "Notices", ii., p. 336.

2) "Notices", i., p. 296.

3) "Notices", i., p. 195.

4) Do. p. 297.

5) Colebrooke's "Essays", ii., p. 45.

6) Do.

7) Do.

8) Do.

9) Do.

10) Do.

11) Colebrooke, *u. s.*

12) Do.

m. **Murāri**

n. **Durgagupta**

of which he does not give the names.

There are several treatises subsidiary to this Grammar which are also mentioned by him[1]:

a. **Kātantragaṇadhātu**, commented on by **Rāmanātha** in his **Manoramā**.

b. **Kātantradhātughosha.**

c. **Kātantrashaṭkāraka**, by **Rahasanandin.**

d. **Uṇādivṛitti**, by **Çivadāsa.**

e. **Kātantracatushṭayapradīpa.**

f. **Kātantraçabdamālā.**

g. **Uṇādikosha**, by **Rāmaçarman**[2].

h. **Kārakakaumudī.**

It is impossible for me to do more than call attention here to the very extensive but late literature to which the Kātantra has given birth directly; I can also only briefly indicate systems of grammar which appear to be connected with it rather than with Pāṇini's work. These are:

II. 1. **Vopadeva's Mugdhabodha.** The new school founded by Vopadeva has found much favor in Bengal. It may be safely asserted that the author largely followed the Kātantra[3], and some of his technical terms are abbreviations of those used in that treatise, *e.g.* 'li' from 'liṅga'. Colebrooke thought that Vopadeva got the plan of his grammar from the Kaumudīs[4], but (as we now know) he lived far too early for it to be possible[5] for him to have done so. This grammar is known by several editions, and part at least has been translated. It has given rise to a large literature.

2. **Sārasvata-vyākaraṇa**[6]. The date of this treatise is uncertain, but it is an improvement on Vopadeva's grammar, though it mostly uses Pāṇini's technical terms. In arrangement, however, and some of the terms, it follows the Aindra grammars. Aufrecht says of it: "Sara-

1) Colebrooke, *u. s.*

2) Aufrecht ("Uṇādisūtra", p. xxi.) puts this untrustworthy compilation at the end of the 17th or beginning of the 18th century.

3) Westergaard "Radices", p. iv., and see above p. 37.

4) "Essays" ii., 15: "It .... proceeds upon a plan grounded on that of the Kaumudīs."

5) The C. on the Prakriyākaumudī, which is by the nephew of the author, quotes the Mugdhabodha. Aufrecht, "Catalogus" p. 161 *b*.

6) Printed with Commentary at Bombay, ç. 1783, etc.

svatīsūtrarum auctor quum grammaticam tironum in usum componere vellet, in rerum dispositione a Pāṇini differt, eamque fere viam ingressus est, quam Rāmacandra, Vopadeva, alii secuti sunt. Terminis technicis utitur quidem, rarius tamen quam aut schola Pāṇinīya aut Vopadeva. Literae auxiliares, ubi adhibentur, pleraeque a Pāṇini mutuum sumtae, accentum indicantes omissa sunt. Litera eodem atque a Vopadeva ordine dispositae sunt . . . . Casuum et verbi terminationes ut apud Vopadevam significantur. Saepissime tamen varia suffixa sine literis auxiliaribus traduntur[1]."

There are commentaries by

a. Anubhūtisvarūpācārya.

b. Puñjarāja[2].

c. Rāmacandrāçrama; called Siddhāntacandrikā.

The relation of the Mugdhabodha and Sārasvatavyākaraṇa to the older grammars is singular; they both have preserved the form and many of the terms of the Aindra system, but have added to it more or less of imitations of Pāṇini's algebraic system, including a modified arrangement of the Çivasūtras which Vopadeva probably invented, and in which he has carried much further the re-arrangement of the Çivasūtras as begun by Jinendra and the later Çākaṭāyana[3]; these last, on the other hand, have utterly given up the old form or system, and have scarcely preserved a trace of the old terms. In technicality they out-do Pāṇini.

There is yet another grammar which may in some respects be affiliated to the Aindra School, but which appears to have entirely escaped the notice of scholars. It is contained in a few chapters near the end of the Agnipurāṇa which is an immense collection of small treatises on all possible subjects, including law, prosody, war, etc. The only MS[4]. accessible to me is so corrupt that I can hardly give even a brief notice of it. It is related by Skanda who appears to attribute it to Kātyāyana[5]. The first chapter contains Pāṇini's Çivasūtras, the others treat of Sandhi, inflection, etc. but in a simple and natural order, and use many of the old (or Aindra) terms. Uncertain as my only MS. is, it would be impossible to say more, with safety, of this interesting fragment. The whole Purāṇa

1) Aufrecht, "Catalogus" p. 172 *a*.

2) E. I. H. 859 written in 1617 (Aufrecht, "Catalogus", p. 172 *b*).

3) See the discussion on these treatises in the Appendix.

4) Tanjore, 1565.

5) The first verse is: Vaxye vyākaraṇasāram siddhaçabdasvarūpakam |
Kātyāyano (MS. °na) vibodhāya bālānām (yad?) adhāraya(t) ||

will, shortly, be accessible[1]; it is one of the most peculiar and interesting of its class, and gives much information that cannot be found except, perhaps, in some of the astrological treatises.

e. **Foreign grammars modelled on the Sanskrit Aindra treatises A. Tamiḻ.**

The most important application of the Aindra system of grammar to a foreign language, is undoubtedly to Tamiḻ. Mention is made of a number of early works—by Aɣattiyan (Agastya), who is said to have been the first Tamiḻ grammarian, and his pupils[2]—including the author of the

1. **Tolkâppiyam,** who is known as Tolkāppiyan, but (except a few doubtful quotations) only this last exists at present[3]. On this there are several commentaries by—

a. Iḷambūraṇar, called Iḷambūraṇam. On the first two divisions only. By

b. Naššiṉārkkiniyar, called Naššiṉārkkiniyam. This is a commentary on the entire treatise, but only part has, as yet, been printed. By

c. Šenāvaraiyar, called Šenāvaraiyam. This is said to be on the second book only. I may notice also

d. The Tolkāppiyaššūttiravirutti (on i., 1, 1 only) by Šivañāṉaδešiɣar.

But Tolkāppiyan's treatise has long been superseded by the popular

2. **Nannûl.** Little is known about the origin of this work; the introduction proves the author to have been a Jain, and he dedicates it to somebody named Šiyaɣañɣan who is said to have been a petty chieftain near Madura, and who, therefore, probably lived after the fall of the old Pāṇḍiya kingdom in the 14th century. Had there been a Pāṇḍiyan, the author would have certainly dedicated it to him. He also mentions his own name—Pavaṇanδi—and says that he was the son of Sanmaδimuni, and that he lived in a town called Šanaɣai which has not been traced. It is very unlikely that this treatise is more than five hundred years old, but it is *the* Tamiḻ grammar. It is much more technical than Tolkāppiyan's work, and has far more Sanskrit in it. It has exercised the ingenuity of a number of commentators down to the present time; but these authors evidently did not know the real source of Tamiḻ grammar, and

1) An edition is already begun in the Bibl. Indica.

2) See the long list of names in Babington's translation of Beschi's "Šen-Tamiḻ Grammar", introduction. The beginning of Tamiḻ grammar must be about the 8th cent. A. D.

3) I have, above, discussed the terms used in it etc.

have often misunderstood the system and terms; their works are, for the most part, insufferably prolix, and contain but little of value. The most important are:

a. Šamaṇamunivar; his commentary is only known by quotations.

b. Šaṅɣaranamaššivāyar; he was a native of Tinnevelly, but became a Çaiva Sannyāsi at the maṭha of Tiruvāvaḍuðurai (between Mayaveram and Combaconum) a great seat of Tamiḻ learning. Extracts have been given by Mr. Joyes in his excellent edition and translation of part of the Nannūl.

c. Šivañānaðešiɣar; of Conjeveram, but a member of the same society.

d. Vaittiyanāðar; a member of the Tarumapura maṭha. He himself wrote a Tamiḻ grammar (Ilakkaṇaviḷakkam) in which he improved on his predecessors[1].

The later history of Tamiḻ grammar is not of importance here. The science has been chiefly kept up by Tamiḻ people of the so-called Çūdra castes, and they have always (being themselves ignorant of Sanskrit) delighted in asserting the independence of the Tamiḻ grammar and literary culture in opposition to the Brahmans who asserted the contrary, often in too positive a manner. Most of the later works on the Tamiḻ grammar are difficult to find, as but few have been printed, and nearly all have only local reputations. I shall not attempt here to say more about them.

It is perhaps worth while to point out that the ultimate source of the earliest Tamiḻ grammar must be a Sanskrit, and not a Pali original. As far as the Sanskrit words go, it is impossible to prove this, for in Tamiḻ they assume much the same if not the identical form that they have in Pali. But I have shown elsewhere[2] that in the 7th century A. D. the predominant sect in S. India was that of the Nirgranthas or Digambara Jains, and Tolkāppiyan was most probably of this sect. He is sometimes said to have been a Buddhist, and the Jains were in fact, heretical Buddhists. Now the S. Indian Jains have a peculiar literature that is either in Sanskrit or in Vernacular languages (Tamiḻ and Canarese). They have never used Pali, and the few Prakrit books they have, are late importations from N. India. The Tamiḻ grammar shows no certain trace of Prakrit influences; thus only a Sanskrit origin for it can be allowed.

---

1) It has been printed. For this and the numerous editions of the Nannūl and similar works, see Murdoch's Catalogue of printed Tamiḻ books.

2) "*Indian Antiquary*" i., p. 310 *note*. "Elements of S. Indian Palæography" p. 39 *note*.

The few names that are mentioned are also Sanskrit rather than Pali—Aγattiyan (Agastya), Āttireyan (Ātreya), etc.

Paγu-paδam and Paγā-paδam (=iṅgya and aniṅgya) also show that the original followed by Tolkāppiyan was Sanskrit; such terms do not occur in Pali Grammar[1].

This doubtful origin is only possible as far as the older grammar is concerned; that the author of the Nannūl had Sanskrit treatises, and especially the Kātantra, before him, every page proves conclusively. It is unnecessary to call attention to more than his rules for converting Sanskrit words into Tamiḻ[2].

B. Canarese Grammar.

It is possible to speak of the Canarese Grammar with considerable certainty, as Mr. Kittel has published a critical edition of the most important which is also, probably, the oldest existing treatise:

1. **Çabdamaṇidarpaṇa**, by Keçirāja or Keçava. The author was probably a Jain[3], and lived about the end of the twelfth century[4]. It is remarkable that this treatise is nearly all in metre, though aphoristic in style, and the author himself speaks of his 'sūtras'; it is in eight chapters. The first treats of phonetics. For letters he uses as names 'axara' and 'varṇa'; 'svara' for vowels; 'sandhyaxara' for diphthongs. Except a and ā, vowels are 'nāmin'. Consonants he terms 'vyañjana'. A theme (prakṛiti) is either nominal—'liṅga', or verbal—'dhātu'; by the addition of 'vibhakti' (both nominal and verbal) or by a 'pratyaya' it becomes a pada. The second chapter is on nouns. The seven cases of declension of a noun (nāman) are 'prathama', 'dvitīya', etc. The eighth, or vocative, is called 'āmantraṇa' or 'sambuddhi'. Chapter 3 is on compounds—'samāsa'; and chapter 4 is on derivative nouns—'taddhita'. Chapter 5 is on verbs—'ākhyāta'; tenses ('kāla') have persons—'purusha', and are 'vartamāna' or present, 'bhāvi' or future, 'bhūta' or past, and 'vidhi' or imperative. Chapter 6 is on roots; chapter 7 on corrupt Sanskrit words (tadbhava); and the last chapter is on particles—'avyaya'. Thus throughout, the arrangement and technical terms closely follow the

1) See above, p. 13.

2) Pt. iii., sūtras xix-xxiii. There was much intercourse between the Singhalese and S. Indian Buddhists in the 12th century A. D., and especially under king Parākrama i., and at this time the Singhalese appear to have become acquainted with the Kātantra and Sanskrit sources. (D'Alwis "Descriptive Catalogue", i., pp. 179-180. "Mahavanso", ch. 77 etc.)

3) See Mr. Kittel's Introduction, p. xxi.

4) Do. p. xxvi.

Aindra system. The form of the numerous Sanskrit words indicates an original in that language.

The author himself wrote an explanation of his work:

a. Arthavṛitti[1]. Keçirāja was not the first Canarese grammarian[2]; but nothing precise is known of his predecessors. The chief commentary on his treatise is relatively modern[3]; it has also been edited by Mr. Kittel, it is called

b. Vyākhyāna; and is by Nishṭhūra Sañjayya, who must have lived in comparatively recent times.

There is a treatise on Canarese Grammar written in Sanskrit sūtras:

2. **Çabdânuçâsana** (in four pādas), by an anonymous author. On it there is also a vṛitti in Sanskrit:

a. Bhāshāmañjarī, by Bhaṭṭākalaṅka. As Mr. Kittel has shown[4], this little work is anterior to Nishṭhūra Sañjayya (who quotes it), but probably later than Keçava. As far as I have seen quotations from it, it belongs also to the Aindra School, but I cannot say for certain. Mr. Kittel considers that it is based on an abridged recension of the Çabdamaṇidarpaṇa, though it differs in some details[5]. The name of the commentator—Bhaṭṭākalaṅka—is clearly Jain; from the style of his work (as in the quotation given by Mr. Kittel) I should infer that he is the author of the text. Vṛittis by the authors of later sūtra works and explaining their own rules, are far from uncommon in Sanskrit literature.

The great and real merit of the Çabdamaṇidarpaṇa is that it bases the rules on independent research and the usage of writers of repute[6]; in this way it is far ahead of the Tamiḻ and Telugu treatises which are much occupied with vain scholastic disputations.

C. Tibetan Grammar.

Even out of India the Aindra Grammar shows itself as an agent of literary culture. The Tibetans have transferred to their larger collection—the Bstan-hygur—a considerable part of the Sanskrit grammatical literature which they have translated in their usual mechanical way[7]. Among these are the following Sanskrit Aindra treatises:

1) See Mr. Kittel's Introduction. P. 5 (sūtra 6).
2) Do. p. xvi.
3) Do. p. xiv.
4) Do. do.
5) Do. p. xv.
6) Do. pp. xvi. ffg.
7) This has been already exemplified by Schiefner ("Bulletin Historico-Philologique de l'Académie de St. Pétersburg" iv., p. 296 *note* etc.) I have pointed out another in Tāranātha, viz., Kumārila (a diminutive regularly formed from Kumāra) translated as if it were Kumāralīlā. ("*Indian Antiquary*" i., p. 310 *n.*) But such defects do not seriously affect the great value of the Tibetan translations in respect of Indian research.

3·612. **Kalâpasûtra.** (Tib.) Ḳ a l ā p a 'i m d o. *f.* 86, called by C. Sgra'i bstan-bčos Kalāpa. *i. e.* Çabdaçāstra or Vyākaraṇaçāstra.

3·613. **Kalâpasûtravṛitti.** (Tib.) čha-bsags-kyi mdo 'i grel-pa shes-bya-va, by Durgasiṁha. (Schiefner here remarks that the Tibetan ṭranslates Kalāpa as if from kalā + √ āp.)

3·614. **Kalâpalaghuvṛitti çishyahitanâma.** (Tib.) Kalāpa 'i hgrel-pa ńuń-du-la slob-ma-la phan-pa shes-bya-va, by Paṇḍita Sgrol-va 'i dvań-phyug, which Schiefner considers may be translated by Mukteçvara or Muktasvāmin.

3·723. **Kalâpadhâtusûtra.** (Tib.) Kalāpa 'i byings-kyi mdo[1].

In No. 3·746 we find the Sārasvatavyākaraṇa, though the Mugdha-bodha is, apparently, not included in the collection. The dates of these several Tibetan translations cannot be settled at present with any certainty. They began in the 7th century A. D., but continued for several hundred years.

The Tibetan Grammar is said to have been begun in the 7th century by Paṇḍita Sambodha, whose treatises (also in the 'Bstan-hgyur') are called 'Sum-ču-pa' *i. e.* "the thirty (letters)", and 'Rtags-kyi hjug-pa' *i. e.* "the application of flexions". An immense number of treatises on Tibetan Grammar seem to be in existence, but only a few extracts have, as yet, been published by Schiefner in his "Tibetische Studien[2]". The names of many are to be found in Schmidt's Catalogue of the Tibetan books and MSS. at St. Petersburg; not one even is accessible to me, but if it is permitted to hazard an opinion on mere extracts, it is pretty plain that they follow the Aindra system.

That the Tibetans got their literary culture from Sanskrit needs no proof; a glance at the indexes to the Bkah-hgyur and Bstan-hgyur will show that they only translated the Sanskrit or northern canonical works of the Buddhists, and all the philological treatises (in the last) refer to Sanskrit only.

Dr. Jaeschke has finished his great Tibetan Dictionary; may I, as an old friend and pupil ask him to give us now some specimens of the Tibetan grammatical treatises? He alone can do it.

Though, very unnecessarily, the Tibetans have (like the Tamiḻ grammarians) forced their system of suffixes to nouns into agreement with

---

1) I have taken the above descriptions from Schiefner's article mentioned already. Csoma de Körös (As. Res. xx. pp. 581 ffg.) first gave an imperfect account of these translations.

2) "*Mélanges Asiatiques*" (St. Petersburg) vols. i., pp. 324-394; iii., pp. 12-16.

the Sanskrit eight cases of declension, and have in other points closely adhered to their model system, yet their treatises appears to contain much that is the fruit of original observation, especially with regard to the numerous consonants that are now written but not pronounced, and also with regard to dialectic peculiarities[1].

Except the Chinese, the Tibetans are the only people of that race who have noticed such facts; their works are then of first importance for a study of the Indo-Chinese family of languages.

II. PALI. It has long been known that the Pali grammatical literature is very extensive. Hardy in 1848 (in the Ceylon As. Journal) gave a list of 26 such works. Some of these were first described in Westergaard's Catalogue of the MSS. at Copenhagen, and in 1863, Mr. D'Alwis (in his "Introduction to Kaccāyana's Grammar") gave an admittedly imperfect list of 45 books; but several of these merely treat of particular topics, and are not regular grammars. I can only mention a few to which I am able to refer. The oldest and model grammar is that by

1. **Kaccāyana.** To this reference has been repeatedly made in the preceding pages. Parts of it have been edited by Mr. D'Alwis[2] and Dr. Kuhn[3]; an imperfect edition was brought out by the late F. Mason[4], and an admirable one (with translation) by M. Senart[5]. This last includes the

a. Vutti; which may be put down as the first of the many commentaries on the sūtras. It is not quite certain whether Kaccāyana wrote these explanations or not. The tradition of the Pali grammarians is given as follows:

"Kaccāyanakato yogo,
Vutti ca Saṅghanandino,
Payogo Brahmadattena,
Nyāso Vimalabuddhinā"[6].

---

1) See Jaeschke's "Ueber die Phonetik der Tibetischen Sprache" in "Monats. der Königl. Academie der Wissenschaften zu Berlin" (1864) pp. 176 ffg.

2) "Introduction to Kaccāyana" 8°. Colombo, 1863.

3) "Kaccāyanappakaranae Specimen" 8°. 1869. "Kaccāyanappakaranae Specimen Alterum", 8°. 1871.

4) In the Burmese character, 2 parts 8°. Toungho, 1870.

5) Originally in the "*Journal Asiatique*", and then published separately in 1871.

6) Quoted by Mr. D'Alwis (from the Kaccāyanabhedaṭīkā) in his "Descriptive Catalogue of Sanskrit, Pali and Sinhalese Literary Works". Colombo, 1870. i., p. 52. Also, previously, in his "Introduction".

"The text was made by Kaccāyana, the interpretation is of Saṅghanandi; the examples by Brahmadatta, and the ṅyāsa by Vimalabuddhi." Who the author Kaccāyana was, is as yet quite undetermined; Profr. Weber has discussed[1] the little matter that there is to decide on, and considers that he is not the same as Sāriputta, an opinion in which Mr. D'Alwis now agrees. It is perhaps impossible to solve the question satisfactorily.

Mr. D'Alwis considers that Pāṇini's Grammar was the source of Kaccāyana's[2], but for the reasons I have already given in the former part of this monograph, I cannot accept this view. That some details may be borrowed from Pāṇini by a subsequent redactor of the work, is possible[3], but the six sūtras which are identical in both grammars appear to me to be rather from an older source than either Pāṇini or Kaccāyana; they contain nothing that is peculiar to Pāṇini, and generally agree with what has been shown to be the peculiar feature of the Aindra system. There is nothing in the sūtras to throw doubt on their antiquity, except an anubandha or so, which must have been taken from Pāṇini. Thirty-eight sūtras are, however, admittedly interpolations as the earliest commentaries allow[4] and (as the Ceylon scholiasts admit) there are several sūtras almost identical with those of the Kātantra[5]. To me, at least, it appears probable that both Kaccāyana and the author of the Kātantra have mostly taken these last from a primitive source[6]; but further enquiry (for which I have no space here) is needed to decide the question.

Another objection to the antiquity of Kaccāyana's Grammar has been raised by Mr. D'Alwis[7] which I must here notice. It is that Buddhaghosa (4th century) does not use (in his commentary on the three Piṭakas) Kaccāyana's technical terms, but different ones. It is obvious that no inference can be drawn from this fact, as I have already shown that many of Kaccāyana's terms occur in Pāṇini's sūtras; still more occur in Patañjali,

1) Z. d. d. M. G. xix., pp. 649-666; reprinted in "Indische Streifen" ii., pp. 316-348. This has been translated into English.

2) "Introduction", p. xi. ffg.

3) *e. g.* the use of ṇ to indicate vṛiddhi. As Pāṇini's anubandhas were new (see above p. 40), this must have been copied.

4) D'Alwis "Catalogue", i., pp. 52-3.

5) Kuhn, "Specimen", pp. 17-19.

6) Except 'vā ṇapacce': this is Pāṇinīyan so far as the ṇ is concerned.

7) "Catalogue" p. 68 ffg. It is obvious (see the article by Profr. Childers and L. C. Vijasimha in R. As. S. J. new series, V. pp. 289-302) that Buddhaghosa's Aṭṭhakathā was a compilation from, not a translation, of older works.

and there can, therefore, be no doubt that they belong to a system far older than the 4th century A. D. This is peculiarly the case with the only terms that Mr. D'Alwis mentions as used by Buddhaghosa, viz., the names of cases. Prathamā etc. were all known to Pānini, now for these Buddhaghosa uses paccatta, upayoga, etc.; but it is obvious, I think, that these terms are not really names of cases, and that they are solely intended to express the syntactic relation intended by the cases. Thus for the third case he has 'karaṇa', and for the fourth 'sampadāna' which are used in this way in the grammars[1].

I have made these remarks here, because (owing to deficient materials) I cannot attempt, even in a summary way, to criticize the present condition of a Pali text[2], as I propose to do (in Appendix A.) with some of the Sanskrit Grammars.

M. Senart promises a complete edition of the Pali grammarians, and I need, therefore, only mention briefly a few of them, which will show that the Pali type of the Aindra Grammar is as important as the Sanskrit.

Besides the commentaries (Vutti and Nyāsa) mentioned above, Mr. D'Alwis mentions:

a. Dīpanī, apparently not as yet found.

b. Kaccāyanabhedaṭīkā[3].

Kaccāyana's Grammar has also given rise to a number of treatises:

1. **Mahâsadda**-(*i. e.* çabda)**nîti**; the author of this knew the Kātantra.

2. **Rûpasiddhi**. The author of this professes to have consulted Kaccāyana. He lived while Buddhism still existed on the continent of India[4].

3. **Bâlâvatâra**; edited by Mr. Lee. This is according to Mr. D'Alwis an old treatise, though of uncertain date. It is very brief, and there are several commentaries on it:

a. Pañcikāpadīpa, written in 1455 A. D. There was, however, an older commentary in Singhalese:

b. Gaḍalādeni Saññā[5]. The Balāvatāra was the source whence the earlier European scholars got their notions of Pali Grammar.

4. **Payogasiddhi**; of the 14th century A. D. This is an exceedingly full and valuable grammar.

---

1) Kacc. iii., 6 (*sampadāna*) etc. See also Profr. Childers' Dy.

2) M. Senart (p. 7) promises to treat of Kaccāyana's relation to the Sanskrit originals, and the later development of the Pali grammatical literature. Kaccāyana's Grammar is almost certainly not the original Pali Grammar; at least, in its present form.

3) *u. s.* p. 52.

4) Do. pp. 179-180.

5) Do. p. 80.

5. **Ākhyātapada.** This is a very valuable treatise on verbs, with full explanation of the inflections. It is, thus, not unlike the Sanskrit Mādhavīyadhātuvṛitti of Sāyaṇa.

6. **Dhātumañjūsā**; by Sīlavaṁsa, of unknown date. The author refers to previous Dhātupāṭhas. The order of the classes differs from the Sanskrit, and may perhaps be that followed by Pāṇini's predecessors[1].

Kaccāyana's Grammar has also given rise to a modified system—

Moggallāna's Vyākaraṇa. The author who lived from 1153-1186 A. D. was an inhabitant of Anurādhapura in Ceylon. Mr. D'Alwis has described this treatise[2] at some length.

Grammars based on the Pali
A. *Singhalese Grammar.*

Drawn up on the plan of the Pali Grammar is that of the Singhalese language, for a knowledge of which we have to thank Mr. D'Alwis who has edited the most important and oldest treatise:

Sidat-Saṅgarāva. Colombo, 1853. In a long introduction Mr. D'Alwis has given a valuable history of Singhalese literature. He puts the date of the text between 1266 and 1410 A. D.

B. *Burmese Grammar.*

Mgr. Bigandet appears to state[3] that the Burmese Grammar is based on the Pali[4]: I have no information accessible beyond this statement, but it comes from a most competent authority. Probably the Siamese Grammar is based on the same source, and the few Javanese and Cambodian grammatical terms that I can find are from the Aindra system.

The above brief list of the most important treatises, in seven different languages, which are based more or less completely on the Aindra system, will show that if the fortunes of the oldest system of Sanskrit Grammar have been rather Buddhistic (or heretical) than Brahmanical (or orthodox), yet Pāṇini's great reform did not completely supersede the older system. This is partly to be explained by the circumstances of the time

1) I have transcripts of the whole or part of these three treatises, which I made many years ago from my honoured friend and teacher Dr. Fausböll's copies.

2) *u. s.* pp. 183 ffg.

3) Advertisement to Mason's edition of Kaccāyana—"I look upon it too, as a necessary complement of the Burmese Grammar. No one indeed can master thoroughly the Burmese language unless he possesses a fair knowledge of the Pali."

4) Mason ('Pali Grammar', in English, p. v.) says: "The book (Kaccāyana's Grammar) is said to have been brought to Burmah, A. D. 387, by Buddhaghosa, and the Burmese translation and commentary are ascribed to him."

when Pāṇini appeared as an author. At that time the aim of all literary culture seems to have been victory in formal scholastic disputations, and the object of teachers seems to have been to ensure victory to their pupils by almost mechanical means; hence the sūtra style which put in order the mere heads of the successive arguments in the most concise way, and by thus rendering these notes unintelligible except to the initiated, secrecy powerfully aided their object. The peculiar relations existing in ancient India between a teacher and his pupils would effectually prevent treachery, and so a system like Pāṇini's would long remain a secret in the possession of comparatively few persons. It is thus possible to explain how it happened that it was only after some eight hundred or a thousand years that the older treatises begin to borrow from the Pāṇinīya system[1]; had it been possible, this would have occurred long before, for the Çiva-sūtras and algebraic terms of Pāṇini are too attractive to the Indian mind to be neglected, and they offer many advantages in practice.

In the history of the civilization that has spread in the course of about two thousand five hundred years from the extreme N. W. of India over the whole peninsula, and even to Indo-China and the Malay archipelago, the Aindra system of grammar fills precisely the same place that Priscian's grammar has in the history of Latin civilization. Just as the early Catholic Missionaries in the sixteenth century, who went to Mexico, S. America and Africa, and wrote so many meritorious grammars and vocabularies of the strange languages they there discovered, but in every instance and whatever might be the character of the language, found in it the tenses and cases and parts of speech of Priscian, which, as they imagined, constituted for them a science of Universal Grammar, so the Buddhists—orthodox and heretical—who were the first Indian Missionaries, found in languages of the most opposite character, *e.g.* Tibetan and Tamiḻ, the eight cases (resp. seven and vocative) of the Sanskrit and a fourfold division of words. Both the European and Indian Mis-

---

1) Çākaṭāyana, Vopadeva, etc. It is remarkable that an Aindra treatise (thus Pāṇiniyised) should have appeared at first the best source to Sir W. Jones and others. ("As. Res." i., p. 354.) Forster's Grammar (1810) is based on the Mugdhabodha, and probably Carey's also; the remains of a philosophical arrangement in it attracted attention rather than Pāṇini's technicalities. The earliest grammar by a European (that of P. Paulinus à St. Bartholemeo) is based on a similar source which (in a MS. note in his presentation copy to Anquetil which is now in my possession) he states he got from two Brahmans at Âṅgamala. May not Jinendra, the commentator on the Kāçikā (to Pāṇini's sūtras) and who was a Buddhist, have been the chief means of communicating Pāṇini's system to others than Brahmans?

sionaries applied this system mechanically; the only grammar they both knew was to them a science, and became an imaginary universal grammar. In its beginning, Sanskrit Grammar was derived from an analysis of the facts of the language as was the Latin Grammar, but this false notion of a science of general grammar prevented, both in India and Europe, the analysis of strange languages; this true method has only been introduced in this century chiefly owing to a knowledge of Pāṇini's system. But (if my conclusions are just), the Aindra or older Indian Grammar has had too important a place in eastern literary history to allow of its being neglected with safety in the actual progress of research. For the Aindra (or primitive Sanskrit) Grammar founded the analysis of language; Pāṇini's systematized the results, and since then there was no real progress till German scholars took up this (to Europe) new line of research. If in any line of research, India is, here, original.

APPENDIX A.

In considering the historical development of Sanskrit Literature (which has as yet been done but to a small extent) the only possible way is to compare the contents of books, one with another. But in doing so, no one has thought fit, as yet, to fully enquire whether the texts as we have them can be accepted in their integrity as evidence for particular periods. A general estimate has been formed in many cases of the age of a particular work, but hardly in a single case has there been any attempt made to show under what influences each work has been formed—in short, to ascertain the age of the separate parts.

First, it is necessary to remark the singular circumstances under which most of the standard texts have been delivered to the world. These are nearly all according to the recensions established by various commentators who all lived in S. India, during the middle ages, and which recensions or editions early attained a great reputation all over India partly because of the intrinsic merits of these commentaries, partly because they were the means of founding religious sects which soon spread all over India[1].

Yet most of our editions—in fact, there are only two or three exceptions—are edited entirely from N. Indian Nāgarī MSS., and most of the editors repudiated with scorn any help from the palm-leaf MSS. of the South, a prejudice which is only now beginning to wear away. South India has, in fact, contributed the texts, but N. India the secondary MSS. from which the editions have been made. Here then is a primary reason for not relying too much on the letter of our orthodox standard editions.

Again, it is evident that these commentaries must be taken for what they are worth—very meritorious works in fact, yet *sectarian*; but a critic who now-a-days would understand any particular passage in the traditional

1) It is only necessary to remark that our chief editions of the most important Vedic books follow Çaṅkarācārya and Sāyaṇa, and that Mallinātha's recension is followed for Kālidāsa's works. (See Stenzler's "Meghadūta", 1874, pp. iii.-iv.)

collections known as the Vedas and other early texts, may not rely on sectarian commentators. The works of such are chiefly of value for a history of dogma, an interesting matter in itself, but quite foreign to critical purposes. Such primitive texts as the Vedas are peculiarly liable to misunderstandings, and it will often be found that commentators only pretend to understand them "because they have grown accustomed to misunderstand them". It must be again asked if, besides unintentional perversions, texts may not have been arranged, selected or interpolated wilfully for certain purposes?

It appears to me that it is possible to establish some general principles, by which Sanskrit texts may be compared for historical purposes; it was necessary to raise the question in order to show that it is possible to use the grammatical texts in this way as Goldstücker did, and as I have attempted to do in the preceding monograph. If we know some at least, of the laws which regulate the reflection of an object, we may, to some extent, infer as to the nature of that object, though it be not directly accessible.

Before dealing with the grammatical treatises, it will be best to see what conclusion other texts point to. The earliest relics of Indian literary culture—the Vedas—are not of direct importance in this enquiry, but it is necessary to notice their present condition and the indigenous views regarding them.

The true nature of the Vedic collections is well pointed out by Profr. Roth. He says[1]: "Es ist eine bekannte Sache, dass die verschiedenen Sammlungen alter Lieder, Sprüche, Formeln u. s. w. welche jede durch eine besondere Benennung unterschieden unter dem gemeinsamen Namen der Veden überliefert sind, nicht die einzigen ihrer Art waren. Jede dieser Gattungen hatte ihre Arten. Wie in Religionsgemeinden, deren Bestand auf eine Verkündigung oder Lehre zurückgeht, die Feststellung des Inhalts dieser Lehre, da sie nicht bei allen und überall dieselben Wege geht, zu verschiedenen Dogmen und dadurch zu Secten führt, so haben sich in Indien ähnliche Unterscheidungen, wenn auch mehr äusserlicher und darum weniger feindlicher Art, an der heiligen Überlieferung entwickelt und befestigt.

"Die vier Veden, in welche der gesammte Stoff dieser Überlieferung seit alter Zeit zerlegt wird: Lieder, Gesänge, Opfersprüche, Wünsche und Verwünschungen (carmina, incantamenta, devotiones) sind ursprünglich

1) "Der Atharvaveda in Kaschmir", pp. 9-10.

nicht eben so viel Bücher, sondern Bezeichnungen von vier Gattungen des überlieferten Wortes, welche lange Zeit nur im Gedächtniss von Geschlecht zu Geschlecht fortgepflanzt wurden. Sobald aber aus einer dieser Gattungen eine bestimmte Auswahl getroffen und nach Aufeinanderfolge, Zahl und Wortlaut der einzelnen Stücke festgestellt wurde—was nach meinen Begriffen nur mit Hilfe der Schrift wirksam geschehen konnte—so entstand ein vedisches Buch. Traf ein anderer Kenner und Lehrer aus derselben Gattung des Überlieferten eine im einzelnen abweichende Wahl und setzte dieselbe in seinem Kreise in Wirksamkeit, ...so standen zwei Bücher nebeneinander, welche einen und denselben Veda enthielten, beide aus derselben Tradition erwachsen waren wie zwei Zweige eines Baumes.......Es lässt sich annehmen, dass unter gegebenen Verhältnissen diese Unterschiede sich zu wirklichen Spaltungen erweitern konnten; in der Regel jedoch sind sie sehr harmlos, ja so gut wie bedeutungslos."

The Indian view of the Vedic texts is remarkable; they are considered to have existed from eternity and to have been uncreated[1]. Thus, the real 'forms' or types which exist in a higher world (like the Platonic ideas), had representatives, but not necessarily perfect, on this earth. As the Vedic texts[2] now exist, they are of little importance for the present matter, but the old Indian doctrine concerning them is of much importance, as it has been extended to other parts of the Sanskrit literature.

---

1) Singularly enough some of the Muhammadan (Sunni) teachers taught exactly the same doctrine in respect of the Qorān. On the Indian doctrine see Muir's S. Texts, iii.

2) As we have the Vedic texts at present, they are not free from errors which must have been made at the time of their last revision, or in the pre-historic times of India. So also some stanzas are irrelevant interpolations where they occur, and the proper order has not always been preserved in hymns which are otherwise intact. See Roth "Der Atharvaveda in Kaschmīr," p. 19; and "Siebenzig Lieder des Ṛigveda" *passim*. See also, Benfey—"Einleitung in die Grammatik der Vedischen Sprache" p. 8 ffg.; and his treatise "Die Quantitätsverschiedenheiten in den Saṁhitā- und Pada-Texten der Veden," i., pp. 12, 25. Special researches of the most interesting character are those by Profr. de Gubernatis (in "Annuario della Società Italiana per gli studi Orientali" I. pp. 41-49); Bollensen (in "Orient und Occident," ii., pp. 457 ffg.) But the whole tradition of the Vedic texts as handed down is, beyond doubt, surprisingly accurate [see especially Profr. Max Müller's Ṛigvedasamhitā (translation), i. pp. lxvii. ffg.]; and this is not only the case with the Saṁhitās but also in many cases with the later Brāhmaṇas. Some, however, have undergone revision (see my "Sāmavidhāna Br." i., pp. x., ffg. in which M. Barth concurs—"Revue Critique" 1873, No. 44, p. 282). I have in another place ("Devatādhyāya Br." Preface, p. xi.) attempted to show that some Brāhmaṇas were put in their present order by Sāyaṇa, and that he must be considered as the final author of the Vedic canon; on this see M. Barth's article in the "Revue Critique" No. 12 of 1874, p. 179.

Thus Patañjali says:[1] "Bṛihaspatir Indrāya divyavarshasahasra*m* pratipadoktānā*m* çabdānā*m* çabdapārāyaṇa*m* provāca nā 'nta*m* jagāma | Bṛihaspatiç ca pravaktā Indraç cā 'dhyetā, divya*m* varshasahasram adhyayanakāla*h* | na cā 'nta*m* jagāma" etc. This is the 'ideal' science; to meet actual wants of mortals we have 'grammar'. A little reflection will show that this view must necessarily hold good in respect of all 'çāstras', and hence, that with treatises which profess to come originally by revelation it is not possible to expect an exact reproduction of a primitive text, for there probably never was one; rather, the oldest treatises we have, are to be looked on as the joint work of many generations of teachers and pupils, and the result of much revision. The Indian view is given by Colebrooke[2]: "It is a received and well grounded opinion of the learned in India that no book is altogether safe from changes and interpolations until it have been commented: but when once a gloss has been published, no fabrication could afterwards succeed; because the perpetual commentary notices every passage, and, in general, explains every word." But there are comparatively few such commentaries, and very few of a remote date, and there is often reason to believe that these have caused in effect, the loss of different recensions[3], which not being protected by such a useful aid, have fallen into neglect. As I have already remarked, such commentaries[4] often originated new errors in addition to those already existing in the texts.

1) Benares lithog. ed. i., ff. 10 *b*.-11 *a*. See in the magnificent photo-zincograph edition issued by the India Office, p. 14, of vol. i.

2) "Essays" i., pp. 98-9.

3) See my "Sāmavidhānabrāhmaṇa" i., pp. xxxiii.-xxxiv.

4) Burnouf ["Bhāgavatapurāṇa", ii. (folio ed.) pp. vi.-vii.] already in 1844, protested against a servile adherence to the Commentaries. He says: "J'ai continué à accorder une assez grande confiance au commentaire de Çrīdhara Svāmin, qui est en général ample et exact. Je l'ai suivi principalement toutes les fois qu'il a été question d'un point de fait ou de doctrine; dans les passages purement poétiques, je me suis permis plus de liberté. Ce n'est pas que je pense que nous devions abjurer le sens commun et la connaisance que nous avons acquise de la langue sanscrite, pour nous soumettre en aveugles aux explications souvent mesquines et erronées des commentateurs indigènes; mais je suis d'avis que leurs opinions mériteront toujours une attention particulière . . . . . Enfin, la condescendance qu'on peut avoir pour leurs opinions n'exercera jamais sur le progrès européen des études indiennes une très-fâcheuse influence; car, de deux choses l'une: ou les explications brahmaniques sont vraies, et alors elles (vii.) se justifieront plus tard d'elles-mêmes; ou elles sont fausses, et alors la critique ne tardera pas à posséder les moyens d'en faire justice. Qui aurait le courage de reprocher au digne et à jamais regrettable Frédéric Rosen d'avoir suivi, un peu servilement peut-être, les sentiments des commentateurs indiens? et qui, d'un autre côté, pourrait être blâmé d'opposer à ces sentiments quelques-unes de ces interprétations simples et fécondes, qui sortent si naturellement des textes expliqués par les seuls secours de la philologie?" This is Profr. Max Müller's view.

Thus, it is evident, it will not be safe to start with an assumption that the later Sanskrit texts have been preserved from interpolations, or that we can look back in hopes of arriving at a text as originally written by its author; in this they form a striking contrast to the Vedic collections.

1. The current texts of the epic poems fully support this view.

a. **Râmâyaṇa.** It has long been known that two chief recensions at least of this epic are in existence; the texts of which agree generally in substance but very little in language and expression. The existence of the second recension[1] which is generally accepted as the oldest and best, was first established by A. W. von Schlegel in his edition published in 1838; but the many persons who have used the Rāmāyaṇa as an authority for early Indian history and the history of Indian ideas, have (except Dr. Muir) entirely neglected this fact. The most remarkable Essay by Profr. Weber—'On the Rāmāyaṇa'—has excited so much attention that better hopes may be entertained for the future.

As regards the first recension (commonly called Gauḍa) which prevails in Bengal, there is comparatively little information as to its history and eventual origin. It has been edited in full by Gorresio, and in the most splendid style; the first edition (of part only) was by Carey and Marshman, from 1806 to 1810[2]. But, like all the earlier editions, this last was eclectic, and does not always follow the same MS. or any consistent rule. Gorresio's estimate of this recension is as follows: "Il mio giudizio è; che la recensione Gaudana non può essere in nessun modo nata d'una rimutazione, d'un rifacimento della boreale; che essa è al tutto independente da quella, non rilavorata, rimpastata, ma originale, autentica, e degna di fede quanto l'altra, che ella attinse da sorgenti sue proprie, schiette, ed autorevoli, quanto quelle della boreale e rappresenta fedelmente un'altra tradizione del poema—" etc[3]. Of the history of this recension I cannot find any certain traces, but it must be of some age, as Gorresio shows that there have been several commentaries on it[4]. Profr. F. E. Hall, however, considers this recension to be a modern depravation[5].

1) Schlegel's edition i., pp. xxii. ffg. A remarkable MS. of this recension is described by Profr. Aufrecht, "Catalogus" pp. 344-5. Gorresio calls it 'boreale', but it is current all over India, except Bengal, and with slight variations.

2) See p. xvi. of Vol. 1, for Schlegel's justly severe criticisms on this edition; Gorresio (i., p. xix.) concurs.

3) ed. Gorresio, i., pp. xl. ffg. The matter is discussed at length.

4) Do. pp. xxii-xxiii.

5) See his edition of Wilson's Vishṇupurāṇa, ii., p. 190 *note*.

Of the second chief recension which Schlegel brought into notice it is possible to show that it has not been left unaltered. This important information is due to the anonymous author of the oldest commentary that we possess as regards this recension, and which is referred to everywhere as an authority—the Katakaṭīkā. The name given to this work is ominous, the Kataka being the berry of the poisonous strychnine tree which is used in India (so people say) to clear muddy water[1]; but the author has stated, in more than one place, the principles on which he worked. These were first pointed out by Dr. Muir[2]; they are as follows:

1. That a passage is to be rejected which is not in the old copies. And apparently:

2. That a passage is to be rejected, if inconsistent with the rest of the text. The subsequent commentators quote these principles and the precedent of the author of the Katakaṭīkā in justification of their treatment of the text. It is, therefore, obvious that it is impossible to trust very far the text of the commentators, for they clearly state that they have revised the text on principles which are not admitted to be trustworthy by modern critics. Besides these two chief recensions, the MSS. vary greatly in minor details as Profr. Weber has proved.

There is no way of determining the date of the author of the Katakaṭīkā, but there is nothing to indicate that this commentary is older than the revival of Sanskrit studies in the Deccan which dates from the 12th century. As the author invokes Kālahastīça, he must have been a native of the Telugu country.

It is unfortunate that we have none of the older commentaries; for these would throw much light on the actual results of the work of their authors, but it is not difficult to see that as all commentators started with a knowledge of grammar and rhetoric as their means, they would gradually eliminate what they deemed ungrammatical or inconsistent with the rules of the Alaṅkāraçāstra. There is yet another cause which

---

1) See Wilson's Dy. *s. v.* The author says:

Asa*m*gatavyākr̥itipā*m*supaṅkila*m*
Rāmāyaṇatīrthasamuddhr̥itāmr̥itam |
Yogīndravāṇīkatakād vipaṅkila*m*
Sarvopakāraxamam astu sarvadā ||

I quote from the Tanjore MS. The name should rather be "Rāmāyaṇāmr̥itakataka", but the abridged form is also used.

2) "Sanskrit Texts" iv., pp. 180-1.

Profr. Weber first pointed out[1]—the influence of a prevailing rīti or 'style'. Daṇḍin, the author of the Kāvyādarça, and who probably belongs to the 6th century A. D., recognized two such, the Gauḍī (or Northern) and Vaidarbhī (or Southern) rīti. Later writers such as Mammaṭa, Vāmana and others add four—Pāñcālī, Lāṭī, Āvantikā and Māgadhī—all of which came between the two original styles. The descriptions of these various kinds of rīti are often rhetorical and fanciful, but any observant reader of the two recensions of the Rāmāyaṇa and (*e.g.*) a Jain treatise in Sanskrit, will at once notice a marked difference in the style of composition and in the vocabulary of all three. Daṇḍin lays most stress on the rhetorical peculiarities, less on the linguistic; he says[2]:

"Asty aneko girā*m* mārga*h* sūxmabheda*h* parasparam |
Tatra Vaidarbha-Gauḍīyau varṇyete prasphuṭāntarau ||
Çlesha*h* prasāda*h* samatā mādhurya*m* sukumāratā |
Arthavyaktir udāratvam oja*h* kāntisamādhaya*h* ||
Iti Vaidarbhamārgasya prāṇā daçaguṇā*h* smṛitā*h* |
Eshā*m* viparyaya*h* prāyo dṛiçyate[3] Gauḍavartmani ||

Having thus distinguished the two styles, he proceeds to illustrate the peculiarities, but the first only is appreciable:

Çlishṭam aspṛishṭaçaithilyam alpaprāṇāxarottaram |
Çithila*m*[4]; "mālatīmālā lolālikalilā" yathā ||

It is remarkable that the phonetic character here assigned to the Southern style would reduce the alphabet to very nearly the Dravidian phonetic system, and the alleged contrary preference of the aspirates and sibilants (which is a feature so noticeable in the N. Indian vernaculars) indicate that Daṇḍin's remark has a solid foundation[5], though I have not been able to prove it in spite of a careful analysis of the letters in several different passages. I have, however, noticed that the S. recension has, *e. g.*, krūra instead of the Northern ghora. The other alleged peculiarities of the Southern style are not capable of analysis in this way, but they show accurate observation. That the influence of local style must have been powerful is a necessary consequence of the circumstances under which the later Sanskrit

1) "Über das Rāmāyaṇa", p. 76.

2) i., 40-43 of the Bibl. Indica edition (pp. 37-9).

3) Tanjore MS. 10,511*b*. reads laxyate.

4) Do. "çithilā mālatī°" etc.

5) This would tell much against the S. Indian MSS. were they not supported by early commentaries, and were it not an ascertained fact that the copyists of the Peninsula have always been more painfully scrupulous than those of the North.

books were composed. The language was then dead, and cultivated for literary purposes by people of very different races and varied habits. It is difficult to imagine two languages the construction and phonetics of which differ more completely than is the case with Hindī and Tamil̤, and it is easy to see in the perfectly correct and grammatical Sanskrit compositions of writers of these two races that there is a perceptible difference of style, and, the Sanskrit vocabulary being amazingly copious, difference of race has led to the preference of peculiar words in different parts of India, as more harmonious[1]. The authors of N. India have (except in verse) preserved a good deal of the primitive terseness of the oldest Sanskrit prose; the writers of the South (*e.g.* Çaṅkarācārya and Sāyaṇa) are, on the other hand, remarkable for excessively involved and long sentences chiefly constructed by the aid of 'iti' which is there used just like the Tamil̤ 'e*n*ṛu'. The effect of these influences is very remarkably evident in the dialects now spoken by tribes which have emigrated from N. to S. India. The Dakhnī differs from Ūrdu not only by a softer pronunciation but also in construction and vocabulary, and this is still more the case with the dialect of Mahrāṭhī spoken by the silk-weavers of Tanjore who (they say) originally came from Devagiri in the Deccan.

Lastly, come the alterations and interpolations which result from extensive religious movements. Of the earliest period of this nature we know but little; the resulting influences appear to have been eclectic and anti-buddhistic. The most important period, and, in fact, the only one deserving serious notice is that of the reforms originated by Çaṅkarācārya whose Vedānta doctrines are so well known.

The question of such modifications as these, and the results produced by them was first treated by Burnouf in the prefaces[2] to the several volumes of his edition and translation of the Bhāgavata Purāṇa; he there remarked the strong Vaishṇava tendency not only of the Mahābhārata but also of the Bhāgavatapurāṇa, and especially the assimilation of Vishṇu with Nārāyaṇa[3]. The Rāmāyaṇa also displays a strong Vaishṇava tendency[4]. It is evident that this is the natural consequence of the

1) Lassen noticed long ago that the Gauḍa and Southern recensions of the Rāmāyaṇa differed in unessential forms of expression. (Gorresio, i., p. xxxviii.) Schlegel had previously noticed the irregularities of form which are frequent in the Gauḍa recension.

2) He, however, considers that the Mahābhārata and Rāmāyaṇa have escaped to a great extent (vol. iii., p. xxix.).

3) Do. p. xliv. The whole preface to vol. iii. refers to this subject.

4) Weber, "Über das Rāmāyaṇa", pp. 6-7. 59.

vedāntism of Çaṅkarācārya which identifies Vishṇu-Nārāyaṇa with the Supreme Being[1]; this system is by far the most popular in the Peninsula, and has had the most influence in literature. The subsequent Vaishṇava reforms (of Rāmānujācārya and Madhvācārya) came comparatively late, and certainly did not lead to any alterations of texts. The literature to which they gave rise consists chiefly of commentaries on original works the text of which was already settled.

Profr. Weber's researches have brought down the earliest limit of the actual redactions of the Rāmāyaṇa to about the 3rd or 4th century A. D. and considering all the circumstances that he has discussed, it is difficult to refuse to accept this conclusion. The real point of his treatise seems to me, as yet, unanswered; for, though, no doubt, the Rāmāyaṇa has old matter as a foundation, and has incorporated many of the old verses which form the débris of the older Sanskrit literature and which are often met with elsewhere[2], the latest period of redaction can only be considered so long as the text has not been critically separated into its elements.

The causes of interpolation and alteration which I have mentioned above, together with the results of the clerical errors of copyists during several hundreds of years, are quite sufficient to account for the rise of different recensions such as we now find, though originally the Rāmāyaṇa was the work of a real author. It is probable that before it was reduced into the form of a regular book, parts were current in the form of ballads[3].

b. **Mahâbhârata.** Comparatively little attention has been paid to this epic, and (except by a few scholars) the uncritical Calcutta edition is generally quoted. It has been supposed[4] that there is only one recension of the Mahābhārata; but this, I shall show, is a mistake,

1) Hall, "Rational Refutation", p. 199 *note*, and 212 *note*.

2) Burnouf's remarks (Bhāgavata P. i., p. cx.) are worth quoting still. He says: "On commenta les Vedas; on en développa les opinions spéculatives; on rassembla les légendes relatives aux sages dont ces anciens livres faisaient connaître les noms. En un mot, on reproduisit dans un idiome plus facile et plus épuré, les opinions et les croyances dont ces livres, incontestablement antiques, avaient gardé le dépôt. Voilà pourquoi les productions des derniers âges de la littérature sanscrite ont encore un caractère si manifestement ancien. Ces productions sont, pour le fond du moins, de beaucoup antérieures à la date qu'elles portent. Leur forme seule est moderne . . . . . J'en excepte les modifications qu'apportèrent au fonds des croyances vediques les inventions des sectes qui se les partagèrent, pour les développer chacune à sa manière."

3) Cfr. Weber, "Literaturgeschichte", pp. 182-3.

4) Monier Williams, "Indian Wisdom", p. 338. "It should be noticed that the purity of its (*i. e.* the Rāmāyaṇa's) text has been exposed to risks which the longer epic has escaped."

though it will be impossible to give more than general results here, owing to the enormous extent of all texts of the Mahābhārata, and also because I have not a complete copy of the new (or Southern) recension to refer to. The other most marked recension is that which prevails in N. India, and which appears to have been finally settled about the 16th century A. D. by Nīlakaṇṭha's commentary. All the MSS. of the Harivamça to which I have been able to refer, are so nearly alike, that it is pretty certain that this is a comparatively modern work, as has indeed been generally supposed. The Calcutta edition of it represents the current text very fairly.

To give briefly the chief results of such superficial comparison of the two recensions of the Mahābhārata as I have been able hitherto to make, I shall separate the text into three parts according to the evidence in their favour—1) the chief episodes, 2) the shorter, final books, and3) the longer books which are mostly at the beginning.

1. The **Episodes** agree narrowly in all the MSS. As regards the Bhagavadgītā, the very complete commentary of Çaṅkarācārya, the text of which is supported even to the minutest details by subsequent glosses, amply proves that this famous poem is in exactly the same condition now[1] as it was in the 7th century A. D. There were commentaries before Çaṅkara's, but they are not now in existence[2]. Another well known episode—the Nalopākhyāna—presents a few various readings in the grantha MSS., but not one of these is of any importance. The 'Samudramanthana' in the S. recension contains some verses which are not in the Nāgarī MSS.

2. The **shorter final books.** All the MSS. agree fairly well in these books (xvi., xvii., xviii.), though various readings are numerous. The differences in entire Çlokas do not amount to more than five per cent, and these are generally omitted in the N. recension.

3. The **longer books.** These differ to as great an extent as the two chief recensions of the Rāmāyaṇa, they also often differ in the number of their chapters as follows:

---

1) Mr. C. P. Brown had a most careful collation made of Çaṅkarācārya's commentary with Lassen's text; if I recollect rightly, the result was a *single v. l.* of no importance! I am not able, at present, to refer to Mr. Brown's edition (in the Telugu character) which was published at Madras in 1852. This agrees with the results of my own collations.

2) See the passage quoted by Aufrecht—"Catalogus", p. 8. Çaṅkarācārya gives 700 as the number of verses, which is actually the case. Bruce and Grasberger's 'Nala' are eclectic compilations.

		Nāgarī recension	Grantha recension
I.	Ādiparvan	250	248
II.	Sabhā—	111	120
III.	Vana—	306	302
IV.	Virāṭa—	77	77
V.	Udyoga—	200	200
VI.	Bhīshma—	118	118
VII.	Droṇa—	198	198
VIII.	Karṇa—	119	111
IX.	Çalya—	65	67
X.	Sauptika—	26	28
XI.	Strī—	18	19
XII.	Çānti—	364	363
XIII.	Anuçāsana—	252	?
XIV.	Açvamedha—	105	119
XV.	Āçrama—	46	45

The conventional division of the Mahābhārata into 18 books is very unsatisfactory for critical purposes, as it prevents an easy separation of the several parts, and the S. Indian division into 24 is preferable. By this the Ādip. is divided into three (Ādip. = 8 ch.; Āstikap. = 40 ch.; Sambhavap. = 200 ch.), the Çalyap. into two (Çalyap. = 56 ch.; Gadāp. = 11 ch.), the Sauptikap. into three (Sauptikap. = 9 ch.; Aihikap. = 11 ch.; Viçokap. = 8 ch.), and the Çāntip. into two (Rājadharma = 172 ch.; Moxadharma = 191 ch.). Other divisions can be traced.

The following will show the differences between the two recensions such as ordinarily occur. I have chosen a fairly average instance where the texts fairly agree; to show how interpolations occur in the Nāgarī text would need more space than I can give here.

Nāgarī. Ādip. *ch.* xi. 1-7, with which the *ch.* ends:

Ruru*h* | Katha*m* hi*m*sitavānt sarpān ca rājā Janamejaya*h*? |
Sarpā vā hi*m*sitās tena kimartha*m*? dvijasattama! || 1 ||
Kimartha*m* moxitāç cai 'va pannagās tena dhīmatā |
Āstīkena tad ācaxva çrotum icchāmi tatvata*h*. || 2 ||

Ṛishir uvāca | Çroshyasi tva*m* Ruro sarvam āstīkacarita*m* mahat |
Brāhmaṇānā*m* kathayatām ity uktvā 'ntaradhīyata || 3 ||

Sautir uvāca | Ity uktvā 'ntarhite tasmin yogād ṛishivare prabho |
Sambhramāvishṭahṛidayo Rurur mene tad adbhutam || 4 ||

Ruruç cā 'pi vana*m* sarva*m* paryadhāvat samantata*h* |
Tam ṛishi*m* nashṭam anvicchan sa çrānto nyapatad bhuvi || 5 ||

Sa moha*m* parama*m* gatvā nashṭasa*m*jña ivā 'bhavat |
Tad ṛisher vacana*m* tathya*m* cintayāna*h* puna*h* puna*h* || 6 ||

Labdhasa*m*jño Ruruç cā 'sthāt tac cā 'cakhyau pitus tadā |
Pitā cā 'sya tad ākhyāna*m* pṛishṭa*h* sarva*m* nyavedayat || 7 ||

Southern. Ādip. *ch.* viii., end:

Ruru*h* | Katha*m* hi*m*sitavānt sarpān xattriyo Janamejaya*h*? |
Sarpā vā hi*m*sitās tena kimartham? ṛishisattama! || 1 ||

Kimartha*m* moxitās tena pannagāç cai 'va ça*m*sa me |
Āstīkena tad ācaxva çrotum icchāmy açeshata*h* || 2 ||

Ṛishi*h* | Çroshyase tva*m* Ruro vatsa! āstīka*m* carita*m* mahat (*sic*) |
Brāhmaṇānā*m* kathayatām ity uktvā 'ntaradhīyata || 3 ||

Sūta*h* | Rurus tv atha vana*m* sarva*m* paryadhāvat samantata*h* |
Tam ṛishi*m* nashṭam anvicchan sambhrānto nyapatad bhuvi || 4 ||

Labdhasa*m*jño Rurur uttasthau tac cā 'cakhyau pitus tadā |
Pitre tu sarvam ākhyāya ḍuṇḍubhasya vaco 'rthavat || 5 ||

Apṛicchat pitara*m* bhūya*h* so 'sti kasya vacas tathā |
Yat tad ākhyānam akhila*m* ḍuṇḍubhenā 'tha kīrtitam || 6 ||

Tat kīrtyamāna*m* bhagavan çrotum icchāmi tatvata*h* |
Pitā cā 'sya tad ākhyāna*m* pṛishṭa*h* sarva*m* nyavedayat || 7 ||

Nāgarī. Ādip. *ch.* xii., 1:

Çaunaka uvāca | Kimartha*m* rājaçārdūla*h* sa rājā Janamejaya*h* |
Sarpasattreṇa sarpāṇā*m* gato 'nta*m* tad vadasva me! |
Nikhilena tathā tatva*m* Saute! sarvam açeshata*h*! || 1 ||

Āstīkaç ca dvijaçreshṭa*h* kimartha*m* japatā*m* vara*h* |
Moxayām āsa bhujayān pradīptād vasuretasa*h* || 2 ||

Kasya putra*h* sa rājā 'sīt sarpasattra*m* ya āharat |
So ca dvijātipravara*h* kasya putro? 'bhidhatsva me! || 3 ||

Sūta*h* | Mahad āstīkam ākhyāna*m* yad etat procyate budhai*h* |
Sarvam etad açesheṇa çṛiṇu me vadatā*m* vara! || 4 ||

Çaunaka*h* | Çrotum icchāmy açeshe*n*a kathām etā*m* manoramām |
Āstīkasya purā*n*arsher brāhma*n*asya yaçasvina*h* || 5 ||

Sūta uvāca | Itihāsam ima*m* viprā*h* purā*n*a*m* paricaxate |
K*r*ish*n*advaipāyanaprokta*m* Naimishāra*n*yavāsishu || 6 ||

Southern recension. Ādip. *ch.* ix., 1:

(Benediction).

Çaunaka*h* | Kimartha*m* rājaçārdūla*h* sa rājā Janamejaya*h* |
Sarpasattre*n*a sarpā*n*ā*m* gato 'nta*m* tad vadasva me! || 1 ||

Āstīkas tu dvijaçresh*t*a*h* kimartha*m* japatā*m* vara*h* |
Moxayām āsa bhujaṅgān dīptāt tasmād dhutāçanāt || 2 ||

Kasya putra*h* sa rājā 'sīt sarpasattra*m* yathā 'harat |
Sa ca dvijātipravara*h* kasya putro? vadasva tat! || 3 ||

Çrotum icchāmy açeshe*n*a kathām etā*m* manoharām |
Āstīkasya purā*n*asya brāhma*n*asya tapasvina*h* || 4 ||

Sūta*h* | Mahad ākhyānam āstīka*m* yathai 'tad procyate budhai*h* |
Sarvam etad açeshe*n*a ç*r*i*n*u me vadatā*m* vara! || 5 ||

Itihāsam imam v*r*iddhā*h* purā*n*a*m* paricaxate |
K*r*ish*n*advaipāyanaprokta*m* Naimishāra*n*yavāsina*h* || 6 ||

In general, the result of a collation of the two recensions of the Ādiparvan is, that the Nāgarī recension has about ten per cent more çlokas than the S. recension; these çlokas generally form passages wanting in the last. Of the rest of the text, a considerable portion (numerous *vv. ll.* apart) is the same in both; the rest of the text presents çlokas found in the Dev. recension, but with many *vv. ll.* and in a totally different order. The short chapters agree generally in both recensions.

It is obvious that I can do no more here than give the principal results of a long (though, as yet, incomplete) examination of the Tanjore MSS. I hope to give more details in my Catalogue of those MSS. The causes of this present condition of the text of the Mahābhārata appear to be the same that I have already mentioned in respect of the Rāmāya*n*a, and like it, the different recensions of the Mahābhārata appear to have sprung from a text based on a number of ballads, and then subjected to an eclectic revision, thus:

Original collection of ballads.

|

Eclectic text with episodes added to it.

A. N. Recension (Nāgarī), a revision of the longer books, settled finally by Nīlakaṇṭha's Commentary.	B. S. Recension (Grantha), an independent revision of the longer books.

(For Lassen's views, see I. A-K. ii., 499 ffg.)

How long shall we have to wait before we have critical editions of even parts of both these recensions? Even the late Profr. Goldstücker did no more than think of such a task as possible with respect to the Nāgarī recension; had he known of the existence of the S. recension, I doubt if even he would have ventured to think of such a stupendous labour[1].

It is impossible for me here to enter on the question of the condition of the texts of the Purāṇas, because with the exception of two (Bhāgavata and Vaishṇava) they have been hardly studied at all. Both these Purāṇas are preserved in a single recension only, but it must be remarked that the Bhāgavata has been long suspected[2] to be the work of Vopadeva (12th century), and it is thus impossible to expect a variety of recensions especially as the text has been well supported by commentaries. Both strongly support the Vedānta doctrine[3].

But the existence of several recensions of a text is not confined to the epic poetry of India; we find it to be the case with purely literary compositions by historic personages, *e.g.* Kālidāsa; the existence of two recensions of one play, the Çākuntala, has long been known, and they have been discussed by Dr. Pischel in an elaborate essay[4]. He inclines to consider the Bengālī recension to be the best. The existence of different recensions of other dramatic poems is also established. The causes of this are obscure; errors of copyists and the usual causes of various readings are

1) There are about 336 MSS. of the whole or parts of the M. Bh. in the Tanjore Library.

2) See Burnouf's edition (in folio) Vol. i., pp. lii. ffg., where the Indian tracts on its origin are translated in full. Burnouf's conclusions appear to render this attribution to Vopadeva most probable, and this view had already been approved by Colebrooke.

3) As regards the text of the Purāṇas, Sāyaṇa's 'Çankaravilāsa' will give much information, for he there quotes whole chapters from a number of Purāṇas of which he gives the names; he also gives the numbers of the chapters.

4) "De Kālidāsae Çākuntali recensionibus", particula prima, 1870.

insufficient to account for such differences as we find in the Çākuntalā, even though (as in this case) they have been at work for an unusually long period. In all probability these causes are to be sought in the difference of the æsthetic (or rather rhetorical) ideals of the different parts of India, and which have already been mentioned above. Dr. Pischel[1] has severely criticized Profr. Monier Williams' statement that "the bold and nervous phraseology of Kālidāsa has been either emasculated or weakened" which is certainly not what one would expect from the Gauḍa style as defined by Indian rhetoricians[2]; but the long passages in the third act of the Bengālī recension where (says Profr. Monier Williams)—"the love-scene between the king and Çakuntalā has been expanded to five times the length it occupies in the Devanāgarī recension, and the additions are just what an indelicate imagination might be expected to supply[3]"—are certainly interpolations. Dr. Pischel has shown the origin of several of the readings of the Devanāgarī recension, and proved that they are inferior to those of the Bengālī or Gauḍa recension; yet, it is evident that the last-mentioned recension does not present an immaculate text. But there is a third recension, that of the Grantha MSS., which seems preferable to either the Devanāgarī or Gauḍa recensions; if those be taken to represent the result of the action of the Vaidarbha and Gauḍa æsthetical notions upon the original text, it is certain that the Grantha MSS. have preserved many readings preferable to either, and which do not in any way show traces of the Vaidarbha style, though the Grantha text is nearest to the Devanāgarī.

The condition of other Sanskrit books such as the Pañcatantra is yet more remarkable, as identity of form is seldom preserved in the several recensions we have of these texts, and additions to the matter are frequent. At least four texts of the Pañcatantra are known, and Profr. Benfey has discussed these with the greatest care and minuteness[4]. The fourth (which I found in S. India) he considers, is the nearest to the original form[5]. But the Pañcatantra is not the only popular collection of stories which appears in various forms; the Vetālapañcaviṁçatī, Çukasaptatī and others are in the same condition.

An interesting example of the way in which these texts were modified is shown by the Bṛihat Kathāmañjarī of Xemendra, from which Somadeva

1) *u. s.* p. 29.

2) See above, p. 78.

3) "Çakuntalā", 1853. p. viii.

4) Benfey, "Pañcatantra, übersetzt mit Einleitung und Anmerkungen", 2 vol. 8°—1859.

5) The same in the *Academy*, iii., p. 139 (1st April, 1872) and also in the *Allg. Zeitung*.

adapted his Kathāsaritsāgara. Besides improving the bald style of the original, and putting the stories in a better form, Somadeva has done little but change the order of the sections as originally arranged[1]; the matter and frame-work of the collection remain the same. In this case both authors appear to have been natives of N. India; Somadeva lived in Cashmere.

Collections of stanzas (as might be expected) differ in an endless number of ways, but yet the number of verses not common to the various texts is comparatively small. Examples of this are furnished by Hāla's Saptaçataka which has been so carefully examined by Profr. Weber[2], and also by the collection attributed to a Bhartṛihari[3].

Even the Buddhist texts exhibit different recensions, as Profr. Féer has shown to be the case with the Daharasūtra[4].

Thus, alike, books invested with a sacred character as well as ordinary literary works, have not escaped alteration, revision, and modification in many ways.

To multiply examples (as I could easily do) would be useless. The result, so far, of this brief summary of the enquiries into the actual condition of the texts of some of the more important of the different classes of Sanskrit works may be fairly stated thus: they exist in different recensions which have been altered under various influences—religious and eclectic, critical and the like[5]. The necessary conclusion is that it is indispensable to examine closely the texts of the grammatical treatises to see if they have been also modified in any way, or if they form an exception; for before this is determined they cannot be safely used for historical purposes.

It is obvious that grammatical treatises are little likely to be influenced by some of the causes already mentioned; but owing to their in-

---

1) The first 5 books follow the same order in both texts; the others correspond as follows: vi. (Bṛihatk.) = 8 (Kathāsarits.); vii. = 6; viii. = 11; ix. = 12; x. = 18; xi. = 13; xii. = 17; xiii. = 14; xiv. = 7; xv. = 9; xvi. = 10. The short passage I have given above (pp. 2. 3. *notes*) will show the difference of style. See also Dr. Bühler's paper in the *Indian Antiquary*, i. pp. 302 ffg.

2) "Über das Saptaçatakam des Hāla" 1870. "Über d. Saptaç. Hāla" (additions) in Z. d. M. G. xxvi. pp. 735-745. "Zum Saptaç. des Hāla" in the same, xxviii. pp. 345-436.

3) See the 'Bombay Sanskrit Series' edition, pp. 3 ffg.

4) "*Journal Asiatique*" viie. série, iv., pp. 297-368.

5) I think that it is obvious that the religious influences to be traced in the Sanskrit texts noticed above—viz., 1) the eclectic anti-buddhistic, and 2) the earlier Vedānta movements—are of little consequence compared with the rhetorical revisions to which nearly all Indian texts (except the Vedas) have been gradually subjected.

tricate arrangement, it is evident that they are very likely to have been amended and completed almost unconsciously; I shall, therefore, briefly consider what evidence there is as to the state of the texts of these grammatical treatises, and the alterations that may have been made in them.

1. As regards the Çixās, it is only necessary to remark that the Pāṇinīyaçixā exists in two widely different recensions, and that it is probable that the Nāradaçixā is in the same state, and perhaps also the Çixā attributed to Bhāradvāja. The others are known only by name as yet. The brevity of these little treatises leaves small room for criticism, for comparison is hardly possible where there is so little to analyse.

2. The case of the Prātiçākhyas is very different, and the state of these texts has been already ascertained with considerable exactness.

a. **Ṛigvedaprātiçākhya.** Of all the grammatical treatises in Sanskrit that we possess, this remarkable work bears every sign of being a primitive treatise. Written in verse, especially in çlokas—a metre well suited to assist the memory, and certainly used in very early times in India—the construction of the rules is simple, and shows no trace of the ingenuity so remarkable in Pāṇini's sūtras. But with all this, the language is essentially the modern literary Sanskrit, and M. Regnier has assigned very good grounds for believing that parts are accretions as Profr. Whitney appropriately terms them.

Thus as regards the second chapter he says: "Ce qui dans ce chapitre et dans tout le reste de l'ouvrage, laisse le plus à désirer, c'est l'ordre et la méthode, surtout pour les énumérations d'irrégularités. Elles sont, en beaucoup d'endroits, entassées comme au hasard, au lieu d'être rangées soit d'après leur ressemblance ou leur identité, soit dans l'ordre ou les règles ont été données. En outre, quelques-uns des derniers çlokas ne se rapportent pas directement au sujet traité dans le chapitre. C'est une trace de compilation, comme nous en rencontrerons, et en bien plus grand nombre, dans d'autres parties de l'ouvrage."

Again he says of *a.* xiii. (iii., 1): "Le chapitre xiii. est désigné particulièrement par ce nom (Çixāpaṭala) à la fin de la formule qui le clôt.... C'est, entre tous peut-être, celui qui a le plus visiblement le caractère d'une compilation. Les fragments dont il se compose y semblent jetés, vers le milieu surtout, pêle-mêle et sans ordre. On n'a pris aucun soin pour déguiser la diversité d'origine des sûtras et les concilier entre eux; mais, malgré, ce désordre, on pourrait même dire, à certains égards, à cause de ce désordre même, ce chapitre est fort curieux; il expose ...

des opinions diverses, et emprunte des axiomes à plusieurs écoles. Il nous permet de juger, par un example caractéristique, de la terminologie des maîtres antérieurs à Çaunaka, et des progrès qu'avaient faits jusqu'à ce dernier, et peut-être grâce à lui, la précision et la netteté."

Again of the three last chapters he says: "Le chapitre xvii a beaucoup moins d'unité et offre, ainsi que le suivant, de nombreuses traces de compilation. . . . Par leur sujet, comme par leur style et leur forme, ces trois paṭalas se détachent du reste de l'ouvrage, et ressemblent a un traité spécial et complet en lui-même, qu'on[1] aurait rattaché après coup."

These admirable criticisms will show that the Ṛigvedaprātiçākhya is a work gradually built up[1] in its present form; in it, we find that it is said to be a redaction by Çaunaka of a treatise by Çākalya; but though this would (in accordance with the contents) point out that the material is primitive, there is nothing (except the technical style), that would justify the attribution of this Prātiçākhya, as it stands, to a period before Pāṇini. So far as the more important part of the materials goes, this may well be the case, but the language and interpolations render much uncertain. With these reservations it entirely deserves the title given it by Profr. Max Müller "the oldest text book of Vedic phonetics."

That the Ṛigvedaprātiçākhya really does represent a treatise older than Pāṇini has been proved in a remarkable way. Pāṇini quotes Çākalya four times, and Profr. Max Müller shows that these rules are really the same as rules in the Ṛigvedaprātiçākhya. He has also pointed out in it other primitive matter common both to Yāska and Pāṇini. In such a case, and considering Pāṇini's style, it is obviously impossible to expect more than identity of matter. Profr. Goldstücker took a different view, and held that this Prātiçākhya is posterior to Pāṇini. His chief reason is that the Prātiçākhyas are "more complete, and deal much more satisfactorily with their subject-matter than Pāṇini"[2], and that they must, therefore, be subsequent to the latter whose work they "complete and amend". He, however, admitted that there is but little than can be compared[3] in the two, and this little consists of the matter referring to the changes of n into ṇ and s into sh (Ṛigvedapr. ch. v.) and the prolongation of the vowels a, i, u, (chapters vii., viii., and ix.), and a few ana-

---

1) As even Profr. Goldstücker admitted (*Academy*, July 9th 1870. p. 272.) There are also a few probable interpolations, *e. g.*, where Çaunaka's opinion is discussed.

2) Do. p. 271; "Pāṇini's Place," p. 199.

3) "Pāṇini's Place," pp. 198-9.

logous rules in Pāṇini's Grammar. No doubt, here the Prātiçākhya is more complete, but it simply gives all the cases in a particular text of the Ṛigveda, most of which could hardly enter into Pāṇini's scheme of a general grammar of current Sanskrit; for he appears to have simply included so much of the Vedic Grammar as was required for general purposes, and never to have intended a complete grammar of the Vedic dialects, or how is it that we meet with the sūtra 'bahulam chandasi' more than once[1]) and in connection with different topics? Pāṇini must have known by heart the Vedic texts then current, and could have had little difficulty, if he had wished to do so, in writing as complete a Vedic Grammar as the one he has given of Sanskrit. The real cause of Profr. Goldstücker's difficulty is that he assumed that Pāṇini's Grammar is the Vedāṅga vyākaraṇa, whereas in fact the science of grammar in the abstract was intended by this term.

It appears to me that, for these reasons, Profr. Goldstücker's arguments that the Prātiçākhyas are more recent than Pāṇini, and are intended to supplement his Grammar, do not apply to the Ṛigvedaprātiçākhya; of it, we probably have a revision subsequent to Pāṇini, but, there can be little doubt, the greater part of the text and the matter contained in this work are far older[2]). His arguments have much greater force in respect of the three other treatises which belong to the same class[3]).

b. **Taittirîyaprâtiçâkhya.** Profr. Whitney has already[4]) pointed out a number of accretions and interpolations in this treatise, such accretions are chapters xvii., xviii., xxii., xxiii., and xxiv. On the other hand the unusually numerous references to discordant opinions of the authorities are considered by Profr. Whitney to be interpolations made in the text after it "ceased to be a mere body of practical rules for the guidance of a school, and in virtue of its thoroughness and comprehensiveness gained more the character of a phonetic 'treatise' on the Black Yajur Veda, and was used in other schools than that which originated it". Profr. Whitney considers that the sūtras i., 25-7, 60; vii., 13-14;

---

1) It occurs eleven times! Cfr. Benfey's "Einleitung" p. 3.

2) Lassen ("Indische Alterthumskunde" 2nd ed. ii., p. 473) unhesitatingly attributes the Ṛigvedapr. to Çaunaka whose date he puts at 460 B. C.

3) Westergaard (Über den ältesten Zeitraum der Indischen Geschichte p. 67) considers that the Ṛigvedapr. is later than Pāṇini; he grounds this opinion on the character of the versification. Pischel ("De Grammaticis Prācriticis" Theses) upholds this view.

4) See p. 432 of Profr. Whitney's edition of the Taitt. pr.

xiv., 12-13; xv., 6-9; xvi., 24 are interpolations, as they express rules not indispensable to the work, and evidently in wrong places where they interrupt the natural connection. He also considers that the parts referring to prosody are interpolations; this may be so here, but I have already given reasons for believing that prosody was an essential part of the old Sanskrit Grammar.

The Taittirīyaprātiçākhya is composed in a highly developed sūtra style; this is evidence of a revision in comparatively recent times.

c. **Kātyāyanaprātiçākhya.** In addition to the reasons already given for believing that the Ṛigveda and Taittirīya prātiçākhyas are not preserved in their original form, and which apply equally to the Kātyāyanaprātiçākhya, there is, in the case of this last and of the Atharvaprātiçākhya, positive proof that they have been brought into their present form at a period later than Pāṇini; for they show an acquaintance with the anubandhas he uses, and which, Patañjali says, were invented by him. Thus we find tiṅ (i., 27), āṅ (vi., 24 ?), luk (iii., 12), lup (i., 114), et and ot (i., 114; iv., 58) as indicated by Profr. Weber[1], and the first alone of these, tiṅ, is sufficient to place this Prātiçākhya after Pāṇini, as was pointed out by Goldstücker[2].

Profr. Weber also pointed out[3] the close connection between the wording of the sūtras in this Prātiçākhya as compared with Pāṇini's, and Profr. Goldstücker attempted[4] by a minute criticism to show not only that the Kātyāyana to whom this Prātiçākhya is attributed is the same person as the author of the criticisms on Pāṇini's sūtras, but also that he wrote the former before the latter. He assigns two reasons for this view: 1) that the Vārttikas merely include criticisms on sūtras of Pāṇini which were not noticed in the Prātiçākhya, and 2) that some of the Vārttikas are obvious improvements on sūtras in the Prātiçākhya. But an enquiry of this nature is hardly possible at present, nor will it be so for a long time to come.

Profr. Weber considers[5] that chapters vii. and viii. are accretions to the original text; they are obviously intended to make the text of more general application. This Prātiçākhya appears to have originally been

---

1) "Ind. Studien", iv., p. 83.

2) "Pāṇini's Place", p. 207.

3) "Ind. Studien", iv., p. 90.

4) "Pāṇini's Place", pp. 205-6.

5) "Ind. Studien", iv., pp. 321-2 and 327-8.

intended for the Kāṇva recension of the white Yajurveda, but now includes references to the Mādhyandina recension also.

d. **Atharvavedaprâtiçâkhya.** As Profr. Weber first pointed out, this is the most systematic, and therefore, the latest of the Prātiçākhyas[1]. Profr. Whitney does not claim for this text, any more than for the other Prātiçākhyas, freedom from interpolation, and the presence in it of some of Pāṇini's anubandhas shows when it was reduced to its present form.

These are as follows[2]: the particles u and su which are called uń and suń to distinguish them from the exclamation u and the case-ending su. Again it seems likely that in iv., 16 taratamapo*h* is to be read, and the suffix p is then Pāṇinīyan. This Prātiçākhya also uses a large number of gaṇas which is a sign that it is a recent work; its sūtra style is also most highly developed, and can in this respect (unlike the rest) be fully compared with Pāṇini's Grammar.

The result of this survey of the texts of the Prātiçākhyas is, that they have been modified in two ways:

1. By accretions and interpolations intended to make special treatises more general and complete. This is a natural result of the fact that some one out of several such treatises as once existed for each Veda, came in course of time to supersede the others which were neglected and thus became lost. It is impossible to show when the interpolations were made, but it is not possible to believe that it was done at any remote period.

2. By revisions of style chiefly intended to systematize the texts, and also tending to bring them more or less into connection with general grammar. In the case of the Kātyāyanaprātiçākhya and that of the Atharvaveda it is plain that this revision has been effected after Pāṇini's time.

The existence of two recensions at least of Yāska's Nirukta[3] proves that the first of these causes has been at work at that text; of the second I cannot find there any decisive traces.

3. Much the same causes of modification can be traced in the general treatises on grammar.

a. **Pâṇini's "Çabdânuçâsana"** (sūtras). Pāṇini's text has usually been accepted as perfectly immaculate, and Goldstücker's conclusions (in

1) "Ind. Studien," iv., p. 79. Cfr. Profr. Whitney's remarks on pp. 248-9 of his edition.
2) cfr. "Ind. Studien," iv., p. 81 and pp. 193-4 of Profr. Whitney's edition.
3) "Nirukta," ed. Roth. p. iv. Weber, "Indische Streifen," ii., p. 8.

his famous "Pāṇini's Place") assume this to be the case; but, recently, doubts have arisen, and it is no longer possible to accept the sūtras as perfectly free from interpolation or revision. The present views are mostly the consequence of the uncertainty attending the history of Patañjali's great commentary on Pāṇini's sūtras, and the discovery that it supports explicitly only about 1,720 sūtras of the whole number (3,983) that we actually find in Pāṇini[1]. It yet remains to be ascertained how many others can be inferred to have been in existence as implied by undoubted sūtras of Pāṇini, or as quoted in the Mahābhāshya; but a distinction must be made as the condition of the text of the Mahābhāshya is far from certain.

As regards the sūtras of Pāṇini it is certain that at least one revision was effected, and that this revised text as well as the original text of Pāṇini were both in use in the 7th century A. D. For this we have the good authority of Hiouen-Thsang's biographers Hoeï-Li and Yen-Thsong; they say: "Un brâhmane nommé le Richi Po-ni-ni (Pāṇini)..... le rédigea en huit mille çlōkas. C'est l'ouvrage qui est maintenant en usage dans l'Inde. Dans ces derniers temps, un brâhmane l'abrégea encore, à la demande d'un roi de l'Inde du Sud où il était né, et le rédigea en deux mille cinq cents Çlōkas. Cette édition est fort répandue dans les royaumes des frontières; mais les savants de l'Inde ne la savent point"[2]. There must be some mistake here about the number of Çlokas in the two texts, but I see no reason to doubt the existence of two recensions of Pāṇini's sūtras in the 7th century. Hiouen-Thsang's very precise statement is that Pāṇini's treatise contained 1000 Çlokas[3]. Profr. Goldstücker was the first to point out two facts which indicate conclusively that our MSS. of Pāṇini differ in some respects from the original text. These are: 1) that Pāṇini (according to Patañjali and Kaiyaṭa) added certain mute letters to the sūtras, which showed by their numerical value the extent of the adhikāra[4], and 2) that he marked some words in the sūtras with a svarita which served much the same purpose[5]. The extensive

1) Aufrecht ("Catalogus" pp. 158-160) gives details; see also "Ind. Studien", xiii., p. 297, *note*; where Profr. Weber has again examined the question.

2) "Histoire de la vie de Hiouen-Thsang", pp. 165-6.

3) "Mémoires sur les Contrées Occidentales", ii., p. 127.

4) "Pāṇini's Place", p. 50.

5) Do. p. 53. Pāṇini's three ways of marking an adhikāra appear to me to be all founded on reason, and to suit the circumstances of his text. Thus the svarita marks the adhikāra when it extends over few sūtras, the numerical mute letter when it extends over several sūtras, and prāk with an ablative in cases where the extent is still greater.

commentaries now in existence probably caused the discontinuance of the practice of writing these marks, and they no longer are to be found in our MSS. That the earlier commentaries had this source of information, adds immensely to their value.

If we take the actual text of Pāṇini's sūtras, we shall find that it slightly exceeds Hiouen-Thsang's thousand çlokas (granthas), but considering that this statement refers to the text as it was in the 7th century it would not do to take it as evidence of interpolation. What was done in this way must have been done earlier if at all. The evidence of the commentaries being hardly sufficient to support the text of Pāṇini (as I shall shortly demonstrate), the only means of criticism remaining is to examine the internal positive evidence. But it would be obviously unfair to base any conclusion on inconsistensies of form, or use of technical terms or even omissions; for some such defects were easily detected, and exposed by Kātyāyana, and though his criticism may be captious in many instances, yet with such a treatise as Pāṇini's is, perfection cannot be possibly expected. What can be done is to examine narrowly the internal evidence from the historical point of view; but I must here remark that Indian chronology and literary history, notwithstanding the immense progress made during the last thirty years, are too imperfectly known as yet, to allow of much success in the application of this method, especially as one cannot hope to find many historical inconsistencies in a grammatical treatise. Examples of rules are, *e. g.*, well known to be common tradition with the grammarians, and one meets with them everywhere; it would be as unsafe to found any historical conclusions upon such an illusive basis[1], as to debate seriously who the Balbus and Caius were, who (according to the old school of Latin grammars, now happily obsolete) did so many things apparently with a view to perplex little boys in distant countries. With this view, it is impossible to fix the earliest date for such treatises by this means, which may perhaps avail to show the latest date. The question of the state of the text remains.

External historical evidence as to Pāṇini's date does not go far back. The earliest traces are to be found in Çabarasvāmin's commentary[2] on the Mīmā*m*sāsūtras attributed to Jaimini, but as the date of this writer is not known, the earliest trustworthy references are really to be found

1) See Profr. Weber's remarks in "Ind. Studien," xiii., pp. 310-2.

2) *e. g.* on i., 1, 5 (where Pāṇini is mentioned by name); p. 16, Bibl. Indica, ed.

in the works of Çaṅkarācārya[1] who lived in the 7th century A. D., but even here quotations are very rare. Kumārila Bhaṭṭa, on the other hand, does not appear to ever cite Pāṇini. It is not till we come to the S. Indian commentaries on the Vedas by Bhaṭṭa Bhāskara (about 1000 A. D.) and Bharatasvāmin and Sāyaṇa, that we find Pāṇini regularly and consistently quoted. As a general rule it may be stated that the later the commentary, the more frequently is this done. But, it may be remarked, these quotations are often different from the actual wording of Pāṇini, and though, as Profr. Haug long ago pointed out, such quotations are merely intended as indications, and the reader is presumed to know by heart the book quoted; yet it is a pity that editors of Sanskrit texts have not, as a rule, ever noticed the various readings thus furnished, but have corrected their text by the current texts of Pāṇini etc.[2]

The evidence of the commentaries on Pāṇini is not in reality so complete as might be supposed, and only the Mahābhāshya and the Kāçikā can be considered; for Kaiyaṭa's commentary does not go beyond the Mahābhāshya, and the recent work of Nāgojī Bhaṭṭa only supports Kaiyaṭa's ṭikā.

The real nature of the Mahābhāshya was not understood for a long time; it was known by the first edition of Pāṇini (published at Calcutta in 1810 for H. T. Colebrooke and under his direction) that many sūtras were not noticed, but Profr. Weber (in 1849) first pointed out that the Mahābhāshya is far from being a perpetual commentary. Its real scope, as it now exists, is well described by Profr. Aufrecht, who says:

"Patanjalis non tam commentarium perpetuum ad Pāṇinem scribere, quam criticum munus exercere voluit. Quare res ipsas raro attingit, sed quae ad technicam regularum constructionem et formem pertinent, accurate illustrat. Amplam igitur exspatiandi materiam iis offert, qui grammaticorum argutiis delectantur, sed in grammaticas et lexica nostra minor, quam ex tanta mole exspectabas, fructus ex eo redundabit." This peculiar nature of Patañjali's work, renders all reference by him to sūtras which he has passed over in their proper place[3], a safe criterion of their authenticity, for interpolation is less likely to have happened in such a case. Thus the number of sūtras which at first sight seem open to doubt

1) *e. g.* in his C. on the Vedāntasūtra i., 1, 13 and 14 etc.

2) Profr. Max Müller (Ṛigveda, vi., pp. xli. ffg.) has made some excellent remarks on Sāyaṇa's quotations of Pāṇini etc. As Pāṇini is almost exclusively the grammatical authority followed by the commentators, this is really a matter of considerable importance.

3) Profr. Weber "Ind. Studien", xiii., p. 299.

will be considerably reduced, and the residue will be nothing very formidable. It is likely that these interpolations have arisen out of Vārttikas[1].

There are also serious reasons for doubting if the Mahābhāshya is still in its original condition.

Profr. Goldstücker held that there are historical references in the Mahābhāshya which cannot be put earlier than 140-120 B. C.; this is, therefore, the earliest possible date for Patañjali, and all circumstances considered, this is probably near the time when the Mahābhāshya was first composed. But there is a singular passage at the end of the second chapter of Bhartṛihari's Vākyapadīya which was also pointed out by Profr. Goldstücker[2], and has been generally understood to state that the Mahābhāshya had been completely remodelled. The MSS. of the Vākyapadīya are unfortunately imperfect and very incorrect, and it is difficult to affix a precise meaning to the passage in question, and say what was done with the copy of the Mahābhāshya which was obtained from the Deccan[3]. It is singular that the S. of India should in this case also have preserved such an important work, and this, perhaps, explains the fact that the Northern and Southern MSS. of the Mahābhāshya differ to no great extent, though various readings occur.

The Rājataraṅgiṇī (i., 176) relates a revision, at all events, of the text of the Mahābhāshya by the grammarian Candra and others under orders of king Abhimanyu of Cashmere, about the first century A. D.[4]

But, it appears to me that the form of the Mahābhāshya is in itself a convincing proof that the text is not in its original form. That it is highly controversial has already been noticed, but I think that, as it now stands it may be rather taken as a synopsis of arguments for and against the details of Pāṇini's system, and as a controversial manual. No doubt, Kātyāyana criticized Pāṇini, and Patañjali replied in justification of the former, but the Mahābhāshya goes further than this. The first āhnika which contains a long argument as to the utility of grammar etc. and which fills no less than 27 pages in the splendid India Museum facsimile edition, has no parallel in the older commentaries, and certainly is not

---

1) Profr. Aufrecht, after cautioning critics against too hasty a rejection of any sūtras as not belonging to Pāṇini's original text, says: "Vix tamen dubitaverim, quin sūtra plura e vārttikis orta sunt."

2) "Pāṇini's Place", pp. 237-8.

3) Profr. Kielhorn ("*Indian Antiquary*" iii., p. 285) has given this passage with the aid of new MSS. He does not understand it in the way Goldstücker did.

4) Lassen, ii., p. 887. Profr. Kielhorn has taken a different view (I. A. iv., p. 107).

to be expected in a book of the second century before our era, but is just what we find in the controversial literature of the 7th and following centuries A. D.[1] How is it possible to believe that Patañjali himself found it necessary to furnish arguments which would justify the study to which he had devoted his life? Again the whole arrangement and the matter are too systematic and copious for a mere refutation of Kātyāyana, whereas the epigrammatic forms of Kātyāyana's criticisms on Pāṇini point rather to an abridgement of Kātyāyana's words than to quotations. It must not be forgotten that Vārttikas of others besides Kātyāyana are occasionally given[2]. Is it likely that these critics of Pāṇini merely stated their corrections, real or presumed, in the fewest possible words, and did not assign full reasons for their opinions? It thus appears to me that the Mahābhāshya, as it stands, is rather a skilful compilation of the views of Pāṇini's critics and of their refutation by Patañjali than the real text of the original works, and that it has been made with a view to practical polemics.

The excellent Kāçikā fully supports Pāṇini's sūtras as we possess them; but though his excellent commentary must have been in existence before the 12th century A. D., its date is unknown and cannot be very much earlier than that period.

It is thus tolerably plain that there is no reason to believe that Pāṇini's system ever was other than what we find, or that it has been substantially altered; the interpolations (if any) are of sūtras and parts of sūtras[3], and the way this occurred in grammatical treatises is best shown in the Uṇādisūtras which form an appendix to Pāṇini. I shall, accordingly, now proceed to show the state of this text.

f. The **Uṇādisūtras**[4] (Pāṇinīya). The only Uṇādisūtras known till quite recently were those attached to Pāṇini's Grammar and which

1) It is remarkable that Çankarācārya and even Sāyaṇa (C. on the Ṛigveda) give similar justifications of their work. The controversial object of these commentators is very apparent in this as in many other ways.

2) Again, some of these Vārttikas appear to be fragments of verses, and metrical Kārikās are quoted. This looks as if the Mahābh. merely gave quotations from Kātyāyana etc.

3) Profr. Max Müller (*Academy*, August 4th, 1874, p. 156) considers that of some paribhāshās "Pāṇini may hardly have been conscious, others owe their origin decidedly to the after-thoughts of later grammarians"; but as many are presupposed by Pāṇini's system, it is just possible that some may indicate a revision at a subsequent period; Pāṇini, however, must have used a large number of paribhāshās.

4) I follow Profr. Max Müller in writing this word Uṇādi; I find that the S. Indian MSS. have it so; in them the distinction between ṇ and ṇṇ is much clearer than in the Nāgarī character.

were edited by Profr. Aufrecht[1]. These sūtras were attributed by Nāgoji[2] to Çākaṭāyana, and this view seemed probable on the ground that he is known (by Yāska and Patañjali's statements) to have held that "dhātujam nāma". But this ascription was conclusively shown by the late Profr. Goldstücker to be wrong, for as these sūtras exist at present they use throughout Pāṇini's technical terms, and cannot, therefore, be older than that writer[3]. Profr. Goldstücker held Pāṇini himself to be their author; it is obvious that they form a necessary appendix to the grammatical sūtras of Pāṇini, like the Dhātupāṭha, Gaṇapāṭha, Liṅgānuçāsana and the Paribhāshās, but it does not necessarily follow that all these are also by Pāṇini; in their present state they show evidence of gradual additions and also of revision. There are five similar treatises attached to the so-called Çākaṭāyanavyākaraṇa which in most respects agree with those already mentioned as belonging to Pāṇini's Grammar[4]; and it is probable that in course of time others will be discovered which attach themselves to the other chief grammars; such a treatise is the Gaṇaratnamahodadhi which belongs to an, as yet, unknown grammar. There are several Dhātupāṭhas.

That the Pāṇinīya Uṇādisūtras are, in their actual state, interpolated has long been suspected, and can now be proved. Profr. Max Müller was the first to indicate this important fact in his "Ancient Sanskrit Literature"[5]. He there mentioned four suspicious words—jina (iii., 2), stūpa (iii., 25), dīnāra (iii., 140) and tirīṭa (iv., 184). The reasons for suspecting these words are obvious: dīnāra is the Latin word denarius which is impossible in an early treatise like these sūtras; tirīṭa has not been found earlier than Pāṇini; stūpa and jina both are Buddhist words, and probably belong to a period when that religion had spread over India. Profr. Max Müller also pointed out that (as Ujjvaladatta states) the earlier commentaries did not notice the first three words, and that Sāyaṇa and Nṛisimha both omit the last. Profr. Aufrecht has proved[6] other interpolations, *e. g.* mihira (in i., 52), an obviously recent word in Sanskrit[7]. He inferred that the sūtras i., 9, 26, 57-63, 84; iii., 25, 91, 101, 140; iv.,

1) With Ujjvaladatta's C. 8°. 1859.
2) "Pāṇini's Place", p. 176.
3) Do. p. 181.
4) The Uṇādisūtra is in 4 pādas.
5) Second edition, pp. 245 ffg. See also his remarks in the introduction to vol. vi. of the Rigveda, pp. xv. ffg. Sāyaṇa's quotations furnish numerous vv. ll.
6) pp. x., xi. of his edition.
7) p. x. do. It is, however, in the MS. I am going to describe.

155, 185 are later additions. He also pointed out several inconsistencies and errors in the text, but these are hardly a safe evidence of interpolation in a book so artificially arranged as the Uṇādisūtras. Profr. Goldstücker pointed out[1] that Nṛisiṁha's commentary (written 1520 A. D.) furnishes many various readings, and adds six sūtras. It is, thus, plain that the received text of the Pāṇinīya Uṇādi sūtras is not in its original condition; I am, fortunately, able to illustrate this fact by a grantha MS. of the sūtras which furnishes an entirely new recension of the text. This MS. (Tanjore, No. 9,994) is, unfortunately, the only one of this recension to which I can now refer; a few years ago several were in existence, and I have myself seen some of them, now they have been lost[2]. It is written on palmyra leaves, and is probably 150 years old; some of the leaves are damaged. The chief results of a collation of this MS. with Aufrecht's text are as follows:

Pāda i., sūtra 9.	*omitted.*
10.	nic ca.
11.	°shṇihi°
26.	*om.* sthaḥ.
42.	*om.*
52.	*om.* °çushi°
54.	*om.* °sphira°
57-64.	*om.*
67, 69 and 71.	*om.*
84.	khaḍeçca.
103.	*om.*
104.	*om.*
117.	*om.*
119-124.	*om.* 123 occurs in p. v.
140.	*om.*

In this pāda some 10 new sūtras are apparently inserted, and the order of others is changed.

1) "Pāṇini's Place", pp. 160 ffg.

2) During the last 15 years numbers of MSS. have disappeared in S. India owing to neglect. In a few years more, hardly an old MS. will be found; for owing to the wretched cheap editions of the Rāmāyaṇa etc., MSS. of even popular books are not replaced. In this case the press promises to do more harm than good. The Madras editions of Sanskrit books are mostly careless reprints of the Calcutta editions.

As regards the second pāda, both texts agree better:

Pāda ii., 13. *om.* °dṛipi°
33. *om.*
39. *om.* ca.
40. vṛiçcikṛishi(kṛiçibhya*h*)kikan.
46. çāsa inac.
68. *om.* dū*h*.
77. *om.*
93. *om.*
96. °tvashṭṛixattṛiho°
122. *follows* 120.

Three additional sūtras are inserted, and there are a few doubtful vv. ll.

Pāda iii., 25. *doubtful, MS. is injured here.*
28. *om.* °çilp°
29. *om.* °madi°
47. *om.* °nī°
63. *om.*
77. *om.*
83. *om.* āṇako.
87. *om.*

After 105 several sūtras appear to be omitted, but the MS. is here much injured so that it is impossible to draw any safe inferences.

The fourth pāda presents the greater part of the sūtras that we find in Profr. Aufrecht's text, but in an entirely different order. Sūtras 1 and 2 are the same in both, then come two or three which are apparently new, then 75, 76, 80, 81, 82, 83, 85, 86, 87, 88, 89, 94, 95, ? a new sūtra, 97, 98, 90 of Profr. Aufrecht's edition in order. At the end there is less difference, and the last sūtras (from 200 to the end) differ but little. In the rest there are many differences of reading.

The fifth pāda shows in a striking way the growth of the Uṇādisūtras; here we find only the following out of the 70 sūtras in Profr. Aufrecht's edition:

1-5; 8; 9 (?); 10; 11; 55-57; 61; 123 of p. i.; (a new sūtra occurs here); 62; (? a new sūtra); 63; 52; 67; 64; 68-70. The term pāda shows that this fifth chapter must be an accretion.

The above brief summary must suffice; for if I were to notice all the differences of reading and the order of the sūtras, it would be necessary to print the whole text; and taking into consideration the condition of the MS. in some parts, this could only be properly done by a facsimile.

What I have done will make it evident that, after the original compilation of these Uṇādisūtras as a necessary appendix to Pāṇini's Grammar, and whether he was the original author or not, the text has been greatly altered—not in system, but by additions and re-arrangement. It is also evident that the texts of this treatise, as we find them in Profr. Aufrecht's edition and in the grantha MS. described above, have been brought into their present forms not earlier than the first centuries A. D., for the doubtful word m i h i r a is found in both. Dīnāra would more readily find its way into the northern than into the grantha text, and this, perhaps, accounts for its omission in the last.

To enquire into the condition of all the appendixes to Pāṇini's Grammar would require too much space to allow of my doing so here. It will be enough to remark that the uncertain condition of the gaṇas is evident from the different readings given by Böhtlingk; this collection does not appear to be older than the Kāçikā; at least, in the accepted form, but MSS. vary much. The Dhātupāṭha is also open to doubt. The late Profr. Goldstücker remarks of it: "There is the same probability for such additions having been made to the original list (*i. e.* Dhātupāṭha) as in the case of all other gaṇas; and we may fairly, therefore, ascribe the present Dhātupāṭhas to various authors, who also, perhaps, added meanings to the list composed by Pāṇini[1)]".

But the separate existence and uncertain state of these appendixes must have had as a result the preservation of the text of Pāṇini's Grammar in almost its primitive form. For, if the collection of the Paribhāshās in the shape of a distinct treatise may have induced changes in the order of the sūtras, and perhaps alterations in some of the anubandhas, it is obvious that the other collections afford means of incorporating new words and additions such as occur through the growth of language, and this without affecting the original grammar, which, thus, remains a safe standard.

The period during which these accretions and interpolations were made must have ended with the fourth or fifth century A. D. The commentaries which mostly were written some centuries later, display a phase of literary activity that will not admit the supposition of a correction of the text of Pāṇini by additional observation, as their nature is purely scholastic. They do not aim at collecting new facts, for Pāṇini was sup-

1) "Pāṇini's Place", p. 188.

posed to have done all that could be done in this way, and his authority was unquestioned, but they refine and argue upon the merest abstractions. If, by chance, a new fact is mentioned, it is simply for the purposes of argument, and the exceedingly few quotations in the Indian grammatical treatises must strike every reader. As applied to the interpretation of texts, the authority of Pāṇini is supreme, and rarely indeed does one find parallel passages quoted.

I shall now give some account of a treatise which bears the name of a predecessor of Pāṇini and Yāska—Çākaṭāyana—but which has been preserved in a modern re-cast.

g. **Çākaṭāyanavyākaraṇa.** As regards the grammar[1] now known as Çākaṭāyana's it is impossible to say if this text is the one to which Vopadeva referred, but it is not difficult to prove of its present state—

1. That it is more recent than Jinendra's Grammar; and, therefore, *a fortiori*

2. More recent than Pāṇini (as was first seen by Dr. Rost). But yet

3. That it represents the doctrine taught by the real Çākaṭāyana, as quoted by Pāṇini and others.

1. As regards the first proposition, I have already shown (p. 7, *note* 2) that the actual text of Çākaṭāyana quotes an Indra on a particular matter, and that the Jinendra Grammar actually teaches this rule. But it is not perfectly safe to rely on a single fact like this, even though the commentary proves the sūtra in question to belong to the text; I shall therefore show by internal evidence that Jinendra's Grammar is subsequent to Pāṇini's Grammar, and that the actual Çākaṭāyana Grammar has copied Jinendra's. It is not unlikely that Jinendra is the same as Jinendrabuddhi who wrote the commentary (Nyāsa) on the well known Kāçikā vṛitti (to Pāṇini)[2], but whether that be the case or not, his name conclusively shows that he must have lived long subsequent to Pāṇini. If then he has sūtras identical with ones which occur in Pāṇini, it necessarily follows that he has copied. But this is the case. Thus (*e. g.*) we find "sto*h* çcunā çcu*h*"[3] (= Pāṇini viii., 4, 40); "svaritenā 'dhikāra*h*" (i., 2, 5 = P. i., 3, 11); "samartha*h* padavidhi*h*" (i., 3, 1 = P. ii., 1, 1).

1) It contains about 2,230 sūtras in 4 adhyāyas, each containing 4 pādas.

2) Colebrooke mentions that the Kāvyakāmadhenu (by Vopadeva) refers to a Jinendra and a Jinendrabuddhi.

3) The only MSS. of the Jinendravyākaraṇa that I know of, are at Madras, and comprise the sūtras and also a Prayoga apparently by the author. I got some time ago part of the first (to ii., 1); and I have lately received from Profr. Oppert two fragments of the last including sandhi and declension of nouns; my references are, thus, only approximate as far as numbers go.

These sūtras belong to the system of Pāṇini, and, therefore, conclusively show that Jinendra borrowed.

Again it is evident that Jinendra has improved on Pāṇini—

a. In the arrangement of the Çivasūtras;

b. In making some sūtras more precise;

c. In technical terms.

a.) Jinendra allows only 13 Çivasūtras as follows: 1) a, i, u, ṇ; 2) ṛi, k; 3) e, o, ṅ; 4) ai, au, c; 5) h, y, v, r, l, ṇ; 6) ń, m, ṅ, ṇ, n, m; 7) jh, bh, ń; 8) gh, ḍh, dh, sh; 9) j, b, g, ḍ, d, ç; 10) kh, ph, ch, ṭh, th, v; 11) k, p, y; 12) ç, sh, s, a*h*, ⨯ k[1], ⌣ p, r; 13) h, l. The 'Prayoga' says:

Iti pratyāhārasūtrāṇi | ukta*m* ca:

"Syus trayodaça sūtrāṇi tāvantaç cā 'nubandhakā*h* |
Shaṭcatvāri*m*çato varṇā*h*[2] pratyāhārasya saṅgrahe" ||

This arrangement is a slight alteration from Pāṇini's system; Jinendra having thirteen of these sūtras instead of Pāṇini's fourteen; but he has gone still farther in some of the Sa*m*jñāsūtras.

b.) Thus the rule for forming pratyāhāras is in Pāṇini (i., 1, 71): "ādir antyena sahe 'tā"; Jinendra says (i., 1, 1): "sātme 'tā 'di*h*". Again, Pāṇini (i., 1) has: "tulyāsyaprayatna*m* savarṇam"; the corresponding sūtra in Jinendra is (i., 1, 3): "svasthānakriya*m* svam". Again Pāṇini has (i., 3, 1): "bhūvādayo dhātava*h*", for which Jinendra has (i., 2, 1): "bhūvādayo dhu*h*". Again (i., 2, 179): "eko dvir bahuç cai 'kaça*h*" gives slightly abbreviated terms for the three numbers—singular, dual and plural; and these are new technical terms compared with the ekavacana etc. of Pāṇini. So also "idūdeddvir da*h*" (i., 1, 20) = Pāṇini's "īdūdeddvivacana*m* pragṛihyam" (i., 1). Again "yathāsaṅkhyam samā*h*" (i., 2) = Pāṇini's "yathāsaṅkhyam anudeça*h* samānām" (i., 3, 10). Ktaktavatū (i., 1, 26) is for Pāṇini's "ktaktavatū nishṭhā" (i., 1, 26).

c.) Jinendra has added a number of new technical terms, *e. g.*: ep (guṇa); aip (vṛiddhi); ṅa as a name for nasals (i., 1, 6); di ("akarmako di*h*" i., 2, 2); dī (= a syllable of 2 mātrās[3]); dhu (dhātu); pa (= a syllable of 3 mātrās); pra (= a syllable of one mātrā); miṅ (tiṅ); mṛit (= liṅga or

1) The MSS. read a*m* a ⨯ k etc., but it is not possible to see how a*m* can come in here, and as a similar letter is needed, I conclude that it must be an error for a*h*. In this part all the MSS. are evidently corrupt.

2) There are only 42 in the sūtras; do ā, ī, ū and ṛī make up the number?

3) i., 1, 4: "Ākālo 'c pradīpa*h*" = "Ū 3 kālo 'j jhrasvadīrghapluta*h*" (Pāṇini, i., 2, 27).

prātipadika); sva [= "s(a)va(rṇa)"]. Jinendra's "nāçaḥ kham" (i., 1, ?70) is evidently suggested by Pāṇini's "adarçanam lopaḥ" (i., 1, 50).

But, with all this, his grammar has essentially preserved the Pāṇinīyan system and technical terms, and to any one acquainted with those terms, it can offer but little difficulty.

If, now, we look at the current text of Çākaṭāyana, it will be seen—

a. That there is much in common with Jinendra's Grammar, but that the Çākaṭāyana Grammar has also improved on some of the Jinendra sūtras;

b. That in some instances where Jinendra has sūtras identical with ones in Pāṇini, the Çākaṭāyana Grammar has improved on these.

a.) Thus, the actual Çākaṭāyana Grammar has precisely the same sūtras as Jinendra in certain cases; (*e.g.*) the 13 Çivasūtras; "aprayogī 't; eco 'yavāyāv"; "ktaktavatū".

The second of these ("aprayogī 't") is a great improvement on Pāṇini's (i., 3, 2)—"upadeçe 'j anunāsika it"; and the author of the actual Çākaṭāyana can only have copied from Jinendra. In other instances improvements have been made on Jinendra sūtras; such (*e.g.*) are—"sātme 't 'et" (i., 1, 1) = Jinendra's "sātme 'tā 'diḥ"; "svam sthānāsyaikye" (i., 1, 3) = Jinendra's "svasthānakriyam svam" (i., 1, 3); "sūṅ padam" (i., 1, 62) = Jinendra's "supmiṅantam padam" and Pāṇini's "suptiṅantam padam". So again "ekadvibahau" (i., 3, 98) may be compared with the Jinendra's "eko dvir bahuç cai 'kaçaḥ" (i., 2, 179). So the Çākaṭāyanavyākaraṇa has "kriyārtho dhātuḥ" (i., 1, 22) which is an improvement on Jinendra's "bhūvādayo dhuḥ".

b.) But in some cases where Jinendra has exactly copied Pāṇini, the Çākaṭāyana Grammar has adaptations. Such *e.g.* is the sūtra "çcau çcuḥ stoḥ" (i., 1, 137) which corresponds to Pāṇini's and Jinendras "stoḥ çcunā çcuḥ". Again Jinendra modifies slightly Pāṇini's rule about the pragṛihyas ī, ū and e, as has already been shown, but the Çākaṭāyana Grammar effects this by an anubandha g, and has simply (i., 1, 100) "gitaḥ", a sūtra which ends a list of exceptions to the rules of sandhi.

Where Jinendra (following Pāṇini) puts two or more terms (in a samāsa) in the dual and plural respectively, Çākaṭāyana has refined on this and uses only the singular.

That the grammarian who reduced the Çākaṭāyana Grammar to its present form copied largely from Pāṇini is also evident; the greater part of the anubandhas and technical terms are the same in both, and it has been already shown that Pāṇini introduced new anubandhas. Not only this, but very many sūtras and even saṃjñā are identical in Pāṇini and Çākaṭāyana, or show nearly trivial modifications in the last. Dr. Bühler has already compared several such in the paper by him[1] to which I have already referred. It would be useless to give more details here, as such coincidences are only of importance in consequence of Patañjali's statement about the anubandhas used by Pāṇini, which is, by itself, decisive.

Thus, though the Çākaṭāyana Grammar has not entirely copied Jinendra's new technical terms, yet apart from the quotation of the last by the former, there can be no doubt that it is relatively modern not only as compared with Pāṇini, but also as regards Jinendra.

But it may be as well to remark that there are other reasons why it is impossible to accept the actual Çākaṭāyanavyākaraṇa as the original treatise.

As has already been mentioned[2], Profr. Goldstücker has pointed out the great development between Yāska's and Pāṇini's views with regard to nipātas; now, it is incredible that a predecessor of Yāska should enunciate the same doctrine in this respect as Pāṇini does, but this is the case, if we assume the Çākaṭāyanavyākaraṇa to be the real original treatise. Çākaṭāyana even has ti for Pāṇini's gati.

We also find sūtras which have evidently arisen out of the Vārttikas to Pāṇini, *e.g.* "Atharvaṇo 'ṇ"[3].

As in Pāṇini, we find in the Çākaṭāyana Grammar the rules for forming the curious names of Sāma verses as found in the gānas, and other references to the Vedas, and the rule 'svaritenā 'dhikāraḥ' shows that the author knew of the accents, yet he has omitted all practical teaching with reference to this subject; but this never could have been done by the real Çākaṭāyana. Nor would he have neglected the Vedic language.

Many other sūtras are identical, or nearly so, with sūtras of Pāṇini, and contain words which are very unlikely to have been known to the real Çākaṭāyana. Such are: "Yāskāder gotre"[4]; but the grammarian Yāska appears to have been the first to make this name remarkable, and

---

1) In "Orient und Occident," ii., pp. 691 ffg. Had Dr. Bühler been in possession of a complete copy of the Çākaṭāyanavyākaraṇa, I have no doubt that he would have arrived at the same conclusions as I have done here.

2) p. 13 *note*.

3) iii., 2, 151. The C. explains this by Patañjali's words (on P. iv., 3, 133) "Ātharvaṇo dharmaḥ | ātharvaṇa āmnāyaḥ".

4) ii., 4, 109 = Pāṇini, ii., 4, 63.

he quotes Çākaṭāyana. Again: "Çaṇḍikasindhvādiçalāturān ṇyāñchaṇ"[1], which gives Çālāturīya, a well known name of Pāṇini himself; the last might notice such a word, but why should his predecessor Çākaṭāyana do so?

Still more striking instances are: Āryavajra[2] (as the name of a grammarian)—a name of by no means ancient appearance; Vāsudeva and Arjuna[3]; nāstika; etc.[4]—sects which can hardly have been in existence long before Pāṇini; nirvāṇa[5] here unquestionably in the Buddhist sense; mīmā*m*sā[6] according to Goldstücker this word cannot be properly found in Pāṇini; so also we find the sūtra "jīvane 'paṇye[7]" which provides for the formation of names of idols carried about as a means of livelihood but not for sale—hardly an ancient practice; quite as extraordinary are the words Çaka[8] etc., if this treatise be assumed to be by a predecessor of Pāṇini.

In short, the actual Çākaṭāyanavyākaraṇa shows a knowledge of the same literature as Pāṇini and even more. Is this possible except that the text has been revised completely? Negative evidence is, from this point of view, untrustworthy.

There are, besides, yet other considerations which tend to prove that the Çākaṭāyana Grammar, as we have it, is not in its original form. It is now composed, (like the entire Pāṇini's Grammar) of six sections—the sūtras; paribhāshās; gaṇapāṭha; uṇādisūtras; liṅgānuçāsana and dhātupāṭha[9]. Throughout, these sections have the closest relation to the corresponding ones in the Pāṇinīya Grammar, and have no appearance of being the productions of so primitive an author as a predecessor of Yāska. Such a writer would never have found it necessary to make a collection of paribhāshās; if he used any at all, they would have been few, and inserted among the sūtras proper which could hardly be in such an artificial style as is here the case, and which goes beyond even Pāṇini.

---

1) iii., 1, 201 = P. iv., 3, 94.

2) i., 2, 13.

3) iii., 1, 194 = P. iv., 3, 98.

4) iii., 2, 61 — "Daishṭikāstikanāstikā*h*" = P. iv., 4, 60.

5) iv., 1, 249. The C. has "nirvāṇo muni*h*" as an example.

6) ii., 4, 180. "Çixāmīmā*m*sāsāmakramapadād vuc" (C. çixaka*h*; mīmā*m*saka*h*; sāmaka*h*; kramaka*h*; padaka*h*). This sūtra is obviously formed from the Pāṇinīya gaṇa 'kramādi'.

7) iii., 3, 35. The C. has as examples: "Vāsudeva*h*; Çiva*h*; Skanda*h*; Vishṇu*h*."

8) In the usually hopeless confusion with other names which must belong to various periods: ii., 4, 104 etc.

9) I have not got the last, but have all the others.

Again there is no trace of the best quotation that we find from the old Çākaṭāyana, viz.: Patañjali's statement that he said "dhātujam nāma"[1]; a quotation that is supported by Yāska's reference[2] to the opinion of this grammarian on this very point. "Dhātujam nāma" has every appearance of a genuine old sūtra, but it does not occur in the actual Çākaṭāyana any more than in the paribhāshās attached to that text, nor is there anything like it[3].

As regards the attribution of the Uṇādisūtras to Çākaṭāyana[4] there is nothing in our texts to support or contradict the theory. There is simply a single sūtra (iv., 3, 279)—"uṇādayah" and an appendix of sūtras closely resembling those which belong to Pāṇini's Grammar.

Again, the Çākaṭāyana Grammar (as we have it) is called Çabdānuçāsana, and this is the title of Pāṇini's Grammar. But with all this, there can be no doubt that the actual text of Çākaṭāyana represents substantially the grammatical doctrine taught by that very early grammarian; Dr. Bühler has conclusively established this fact.

Thus, Pāṇini quotes Çākaṭāyana in three places:

iii., 4, 111—"Lañah Çākaṭāyanasyai 'va." This corresponds to "āddvishor jher jus vā" in the Çākaṭāyana Grammar (i., 4, 106) as Dr. Bühler has pointed out[5].

viii., 3, 18—"Vyor laghuprayatnatarah Çākaṭāyanasya." Dr. Bühler has pointed out[6] that this is of the same effect as Çākaṭāyana's "Vyoshyā 'ghobhobhagoh" "acy aspashṭaç ca" (i., 1, 153-4). This doctrine is attributed to Çākaṭāyana in the Atharvaprātiçākhya (ii., 24) and also by Ahobala Bhaṭṭa, a late writer.

viii., 4, 50—"Triprabhṛitishu Çākaṭāyanasya." The sūtras i., 1, 117-119 in the Çākaṭāyana Grammar teach in effect this doctrine—"Aco hro hracah". "adīrghāt". "na samyoge"[7].

These coincidences prove that our existing treatise is really based on the original work; it is not likely that an Indian forger would have thought of such details; for, in all particulars, Indian forgeries are most clusmy.

---

1) On Pāṇini, iii., 3, 1.
2) Ed. Roth, p. 31.
3) Other references to Çākaṭāyana are Ṛikpr. i., 3; xiii., 16; but these do not admit of identification.
4) See Goldstücker's "Pāṇini's Place", pp. 171-182.
5) "Orient und Occident", iii., p. 182.
6) Do. ii., pp. 691-2.
7) Do. do. pp. 692-3.

The above facts can hardly leave a doubt as to the origin of the present form of the Çākaṭāyana Grammar—that it is a comparatively modern redaction of an old treatise effected under Jain influences not much earlier than the 12th century A. D., for it is not possible to put Jinendra much earlier than that. This points to the period of Jain revival under the Cālukyas in the N. Deccan and elsewhere, which is already known, and seems to be the only period possessing this character. The most remarkable literary results of it are the now well known works of Hemacandra. The author of the present redaction of Çākaṭāyana's Grammar must have belonged to Central India. His name is not known; the Grammar is said to be by "Çrutakevalideçīya-Çākaṭāyana" or by "Çākaṭāyana almost an arhat." The reason of the redaction is evident—the great place Pāṇini's Grammar occupied in brahmanical studies, and the (to Indians) exceedingly great attractions of his algebraic formulæ. On the other hand, the Jains at such a period would not be content with a brahmanical treatise, but would want one of their own as they had for other matters.

The results of the above enquiry may be thus expressed genealogically:

(Old) Çākaṭāyana Gr. (*c.* 500 A. D.?)

Pāṇini's Gr. (*c.* 300 A. D.)

Jinendra's Gr. (*c.* 1000 A. D?)

(Matter with new additions) (Form with new additions)

(Abhinava) Çākaṭāyana. (*c.* 1100 A. D.?)

I am not in a position to trace quotations from the actual Çākaṭāyana in other Sanskrit grammatical treatises; according to Profr. Goldstücker[1] the Gaṇaratnamahodadhi quotes repeatedly a Çākaṭāyana, but I am unable to refer to that treatise[2]. It is very unlikely that the real Çākaṭāyana Grammar is still in existence.

h. **Kâtantra.** It may now be possible to briefly consider the condition of the text of what appears to me to be the most complete existing representative of the Sanskrit Grammars before Pāṇini—the Kātantra. As Profr. Eggeling, the editor of this text, will, doubtless, soon have much to say on this subject, my remarks will be very brief.

1) "Pāṇini's Place", p. 177.

2) An edition, in every way complete, is to be hoped for from Profr. Eggeling.

A good deal of the Kātantra is in verse and in ordinary çlokas; the rest is in sūtras of the simplest character. This varied style makes it very unlikely that it is now in its original form: it is, probably, a compilation from old sūtras and Kārikās, of which it has preserved much of the original character. The language, also, wants the marks of the earlier periods, and this is an additional reason in favor of the above inference. But a stronger proof that the Kātantra in its present form is not primitive is the presence in it, to a slight extent, of some anubandhas etc. which are peculiar to Pāṇini. These almost exclusively occur in chapters which are modern interpolations made with a view to complete the somewhat scanty text, such as the sections on taddhita and other derivatives (ii., 6; iv., 1-5).

The use of -t to specialize any particular vowel is an invention of Pāṇini, as he defines its use[1]; but this occasionally occurs in the Kātantra[2], and must, therefore, be copied from Pāṇini. So also must ut (as an anubandha)[3] and ṭā[4].

That the Kātantra has been brought into its present form at a period later than Pāṇini is thus certain; but the introduction into the original text of a few of Pāṇini's peculiar technical terms has little changed the primitive character of the treatise, and it is therefore, by reason of its completeness, the best existing representative of the school of grammar which preceded Pāṇini's great work, and which soon became obsolete in N. India and among students of Sanskrit.

The condition of the text of Kaccāyana's Grammar is much the same as that of the Kātantra[5].

The results of the above enquiry are the following.

As regards the condition of the Sanskrit texts that we now possess, it is necessary to distinguish three periods in Indian literary history:—

1. The Vedic or 'pre-historic' period.

The texts which have come down to us from this period were brought into their present form at a period of which we have no knowledge historically. From that time till now they have been handed down with strict accuracy, and the few changes that may be suspected are rather of re-arrangement of matter than alteration of the text.

---

1) "Taparas tatkālasya", i., 1, 70.
2) i., 2, 17; i., 3, 1; ii., 1, 8-9, 63, etc.
3) ii., 1, 6.
4) ii., 1, 23. 53.
5) But it admits the use of various technical terms (i., 1, 3).

2. The second period may be termed that of 'the mythical age' of Indian literature; for, except the little information that is furnished by Greek writers, and what has been gathered from coins and inscriptions, we know nothing about the history of India during this period which may be said to begin about 500 B. C. and lasted down to 700 A. D.

During this period Indian science and epic poetry began, and were perfected, and to this period must be assigned very nearly all that is of permanent interest and value in Sanskrit literature. Texts of works belonging to this period have been repeatedly worked over and for various objects; we have the results, but no information as to how and when these were obtained; and often these results vary in form, though hardly in the contents. Thus (excepting partly the grammatical treatises, for reasons which I shall presently give) it is very hazardous to attempt to use such texts for historical purposes. The most rigid criticism must be applied to the texts before we can safely presume to quote the epic poetry; but it will take years for this to be done, if it ever can or will be done. And it may be safely asserted that the result of such criticism will be to reduce the value of most of the editions that we have, to less than that of an ordinary MS. Pedants have done their worst during centuries, and thus, for historical purposes, there can be no test by language. We may, eventually, be able to say in what part of India a text has been brought to its present form, but an historical standard remains to be discovered[1].

3. The third period may be fairly termed 'historical'. The excellent Chinese pilgrim Hiouen-Thsang who visited India in the 7th century gives us an admirable account of the state of affairs just before the modern Hindu revivals. A few years later Çaṅkarācārya began the period of modern Hinduism, to be followed by many reformers. Since then a chronological history is possible, and this is the best foundation for researches into the earlier periods. When we understand Çaṅkarācārya's teaching, we can hope for some light as to what it was that he succeeded in superseding.

During this period, the Sanskrit texts left by old writers suffered alteration in many cases, and even the works of modern writers did not

1) There is great hope that the movement (set on foot by Dr. Whitley Stokes) for preserving the remaining Sanskrit MSS. may render this possible, but time may not be lost, for in a few years more hardly a MS. will be left anywhere. If carefully preserved, the South-Indian MSS. last a long time, but they are very easily destroyed. Careful people usually hang them up in a crate in the chimney (or what does for a chimney in Indian kitchens), as the smoke keeps off the white ants which infest all wood-work such as shelves. If white ants attack a palm-leaf MS., they can devour it in a few hours.

escape; but it is comparatively easy now to trace out what has been done; and for this period, if a few precautions be observed, texts can safely be used for historical purposes.

Such results will, I fear, little satisfy the majority of those who amuse themselves with Indian antiquities, and who find so many royal roads by which they discover what they wish in the past; but modern critical studies fully bear me out in this respect, at least.

I have already said that I believe that the grammatical treatises are the most accurately preserved of the literary productions of the second or (as I have termed it) the 'mythical' period. My reasons are as follows:

I have shown that the chief influences which have contributed to alter the more important texts of this period, are religious and rhetorical. It is obvious that these influences could have no effect on the grammatical treatises which belong to it. There remain alterations arising out of clerical errors—but these cannot be looked for, as the nature of these texts would not allow any great changes even in commentaries—and alterations in consequence of the adoption of improved technical terms and an improved or more developed system. These last are alone of importance, but there is less room for them than might, at first sight, be supposed. The one notable epoch in Indian grammatical studies was made by Pāṇini, but it was his work to systematize the observations of his predecessors, and this he did by aid of his Çivasūtras and system of anubandhas. This system formed the greatest contrast to the simple philosophical analysis of the Aindra grammarians, and it determined the whole course of Indian grammatical studies for the future. Thus the history of the systems of Sanskrit Grammar shows three stages—1) the primitive, natural (Aindra) system; 2) Pāṇini's artificial system; and, 3) modern adaptations of Pāṇini's system made in historic times.

Any interpolations in the older treatises which have been made after Pāṇini show this by the adoption of symbols or technical terms peculiar to him, and there can be little doubt that what has been done in this way was done before 700 A. D. As regards the text of Pāṇini it will not be safe to use it for other historical purposes, without precautions, for the reasons already given (pp. 88-9); but there is every reason to believe that it is better preserved than any other text except those of the Vedic collections. It will be safe to use it for enquiry into the history of grammatical notions in India, for in this respect there can be no doubt that it is unaltered; but it seems to me unsafe to attempt to make history out of the words which do[1] or do not occur in it; for interpolation of such, being easy, is most probable, and negative evidence, owing to the nature of the treatise, is of little value[2].

If it were proved that the Hindu grammarians really based their works on observation, I should end my remarks here. There is, however, one question remaining which must be asked, though, with regard to these grammarians, it may appear strange—did the Indian grammarians who have done such astonishing work always go by observation, and is there nothing fictitious (apart from symbols, imaginary roots etc.) recorded by them?

It will be safe to answer this in the negative as far as the earliest grammarians are concerned, but with the later writers on this subject, strict scrutiny is necessary; for I am able to give an account of a real grammar of a fictitious Prakrit dialect, called the Bhāṇḍīrabhāshā, which still exists, written in sūtras with a Sanskrit commentary. This curious specimen of Indian pedantry is in the Palace Library at Tanjore; the MS.[3] is on palm-leaves and the character used is Telugu. There is no date to it, but I cannot be far wrong in assigning it to the early part of the 17th century, and it must have been copied from an older MS.[4] The date of the composition is not ascertainable except that the commentary (which is evidently by the author[5]) refers to the Pāṇinīya, Kaumāra, Kātyāyanīya and Jainendra Grammars, and the text may thus be put down as belonging to some period between 1300 and 1500 A. D. It also quotes a Vatsa.

It proceeds like nearly all Prakrit Grammars by assuming the existence of Sanskrit and that its grammar and vocabulary are known, and then gives rules for forming Bhāṇḍīra words from it.

---

1) I have attempted to show that 'Kamboja' must be an interpolation (see my "Elements of S. Indian Palæography" p. 32) on the ground that we find it with other proper names which cannot belong to the same historical period. On this, see Profr. Weber's remarks to the contrary in his review of my book in the "Jenaer Literaturzeitung" (1875, No. 24) p. 418. M. Barth (in his review of the same in the "Revue Critique") is not more favorable to my view, and the matter is doubtful. It is remarkable that allusions to such nations as the Kambojas Yavanas etc. form part of the Indian technical system of poetry, and are regular commonplaces.

2) It need only be recollected that Pāṇini's sūtras were taught orally and committed always to memory.

3) No. 9,997 *ll.* 46. There are 3 other copies—9,996; 9,998; 9,991 and 10,000. No. 10,001 contains a "Bhāṇḍīraliṅganirṇaya"!!

4) For it ends abruptly. If the author went so far as to write what comes to 63 quarto pages of this stuff, there is no reason why he should not finish it.

5) In one place the book is called "Bhāṇḍīravyākaraṇavṛitti" from Vāgīçvara's "Bhāshāmañjarī".

The source of this language (!) is thus given:

> Bhāṇḍīradeçe bhāṇḍīravaṭaçākhāprasārite |
> Bṛindāvanāntare Kṛishṇa*h* pūrṇānandapariplutaḥ ||
> Kāliṅga-Gauḍa-Kāmbhojā 'vantya-Saurāshṭra-Māgadhai*h* ||
> Mahārāshṭre ca sa*m*bhūtai*h* sarasair gopikājanai*h* |
> Tai*h* sahasrai*h* shoḍaçabhi*h* parita*h* paribhūshita*h* ||
> Pariçramam apākartu*m* rāsakrīḍā*m* vidhāya ca |
> Bhāṇḍīratarum āçritya tribhaṅgisthānakasthita*h* ||
> Adha*h*karābhyā*m* pañcamakriyācāturyalolupa*h* ||
> Cārayann ūrdhvapāṇibhyā*m* veṇunāda*m* mṛidutvata*h* (*sic*) |
> Tābhis taddeçajān rāgān ākarṇya parayā mudā ||
> . . . .
> . . . . gopastrīparibhāshitān |
> Mṛidvālāpān samādāya rāgān so 'poshayan mudā ||

Of this, Nārada was ordered by Gopīnātha (*i. e.* Kṛishṇa) to compose a grammar which he did, and which he taught to Çārdūlamuni!

Its character and purpose are given:

> Ghoshāxarair yuktam api mṛidu çrāvya*m* manoharam |
> Prakāçārtha*m* gītayoga*m* bhāṇḍīram iti kathyate ||

It is, therefore, merely intended to suit certain musical purposes, but we find a most elaborate grammar which begins with modified Çivasūtras reduced to eight:

a, i, u, n | ṛi, lṛi, k | e, o, ṅ | ai, au, c | h, y, s, r, l, ṇ |
ń, m, ṅ, ṇ, n, m | jh, bh, gh, ḍh, dh, j, b, g, ḍ, d,
c, ph, ch, ṭh, th, k, p, c, ṭ, t, y | ç, sh, s, t |

It is no real Prakrit that we have to deal with; it seems to be a mechanically formed jargon. A few examples will show the character of the alterations made:

aikhun aikhuni = ākarṇyā 'karṇya.
kṛishṇuv ānanddu = kṛishṇasyā 'nanda*h*.
teṇe ujali = teno 'jjvalitam.
aritu = harita*h*. aruhu = arha*h*. cekkam = cakram.
Haricandaru = Hariçcandra*h*. bhu*m*mi = bhūmi*h*—etc.

As far as I can judge, words are altered in this way to suit the Telugu ear; in that language a final -u is very usual. The C. is here and there in the Telugu language.

Besides this, an elaborate system of inflection for nouns and verbs, is given. Thus: Rāmu = Rāma*h*; Rāmi*m* = Rāmai*h*; and the other cases are much the same as ordinary Prakrit, except that the final vowel seems generally made optional, and the genitive is Rāmāsa as well as Rāmassa.

√Bhū is thus inflected in the present tense:

Singular:	bhomi	*Plural:*	bhoma
	bhosi		bhodha
	bhodi, bhoti		bhonti.

After giving Pāṇini's technical terms for the tenses the writer says: "teshā*m* rūpa*m* Sanskṛitavat sarva*m* tadbhavasa*m*matāt."

It is thus evident that this Bhāṇḍīrabhāshā is merely an artificial variety of Prakrit, but which violates the phonetic rule of the last by which kh, gh, th, dh, bh usually become h.

In the earlier Sanskrit literature there is a tendency to pervert foreign names so as to give them Indian forms or meanings (*e.g.* the Greek Menander[1] and Demetrius have become Milinda and Dattamitra)[2]; and, occasionally, very advanced grammars (*e.g.* Yāska in his explanation of Kamboja) go very far wrong in etymological speculations, and try to turn even foreign words into Sanskrit. But this error arose out of the erroneous notion that all languages were depraved Sanskrit[3], and did not at all resemble such freaks of the imagination as the Bhāṇḍīrabhāshā.

The explanation of the creation of this fictitious language is I think to be sought in the existence of the poetical dialects (kāvya, maṇipravāla, kavi), which originated in the middle ages in S. India and Java, and which consist of a singular mixture of Sanskrit and vernacular words with vernacular inflections for the most part. With artificial jargons of this kind as examples, the invention of a Bhāṇḍīrabhāshā is not incomprehensible.

The intense desire for completeness that we find everywhere in Indian treatises, and which has led to the insertion of impossible cases in treatises on law, and to impracticable sacrifices in the Çrauta-sūtras, may possibly have led the earlier grammarians astray, and they may record some unreal words and forms which analogy suggested to them; but I am not aware that there has been found, as yet, the least reason to believe this. As regards the later times, when grammatical studies had degene-

1) Childers' "Pali Dictionary," p. 247 *s.v.* "Milinda".

2) Weber "Über das Rāmāyaṇa" p. 77.

3) "Elements of South-Indian Palæography," p. 85.

rated into scholasticism, it is possible (as the above example will show) that much recorded is the result of imagination. At all events, all will agree that great care is necessary to sift and test the statements of the later grammarians[1].

But (except as far as I have shown already) the texts on which I have relied in the previous monograph are free from suspicion, and, apart from errors of my own, are perfectly safe premises for argument. I have relied on sūtras of Pāṇini that are supported by Patañjali explicitly or implicitly, and I believe that thus my deductions have a solid foundation.

1) Profr. Kern ("Over de Jaartelling der Zuidelijke Buddhisten", pp. 108 ffg.) has given very strong reasons for considering that the gāthā dialect is no real language; but this dialect is exceptional, and we do not find any traces of it in the grammatical treatises. Where a dead language (it must be recollected) is used, as Latin was in the Midle ages, and as Sanskrit still is in India, such a jargon as the gāthās must be expected; it is, so far, a natural result of the circumstances, and in no way resembles the Bhāṇḍīrabhāshā which is purely artificial. The one occurs when a person attempts to express himself in a strange language which he knows imperfectly; the other is like thieves' cant. At all events the principles which we find in the M. Bhāshya are perfectly sound; it is said there: "ghaṭena kāryam karishyan kumbhakārakulam gatvā 'ha: kuru ghaṭam kāryam anena karishyāmī 'ti. Na tadvac chabdān prayuyuxamāṇo vaiyākaraṇakulam gatvā 'ha 'kuru çabdān prayoxya iti" (I. O. ed. p. 15).

It is difficult to believe that grammarians who wrote thus could have admitted anything questionable.

APPENDIX B.

In the foregoing monograph, I have endeavoured to throw some light on the history of one of the systems of Sanskrit Grammar, and incidentally I have touched on the history of a few of the technical terms used by the grammarians. This last is a very important, but a very extensive and difficult subject; for before it can be successfully attempted, several preliminary points—such as the subject I have here discussed—must be settled, and critical editions of several important texts are yet wanted. I shall now briefly notice a point connected with it—the inflectional treatment by the grammarians of words already inflected or of fictions invented by them. I shall do little but give the results of the notices by M. Regnier[1)] and Profr. Weber[2)] with additions of my own, as my object is merely to show that in this case a perceptible development can be traced which supports the conclusions at which I have arrived. The tendency is to do away gradually with real words, and to substitute fictions in their place; but these are merely nouns, for the technical syntax renders verbs absolutely unnecessary in the later sūtras.

I. As regards **letters.** In the earliest specimens of analysis of the Sanskrit phonetic system that we possess we find

a. **Names of letters.** Such are formed 1) by adding -kāra or -varṇa to the sound; 2) by the unchanged sound itself, *e.g.* a; 3) by adding a or some other vowel to a consonant; 4) by a special name, *e.g.* repha (r); 5) names of classes of letters are also formed by the first of the class followed by -varga.

---

1) "Ṛigveda pr." note on introductory lines to *a*, i.

2) "Ind. Studien" iv., pp. 91-2.

Examples of the first occur in the Brāhmaṇas and the technical words thus formed are treated and inflected like ordinary nouns[1]. Most of these different methods of naming sounds of the Sanskrit alphabet occur in the Prātiçākhyas. Thus:

R̥igvedaprātiçākhya. 1) ka-kāra, etc. (iv. 6). 2) i, u, e, etc. (Introd.) 3) kakhau, etc. (do.) da. 4) repha (i., 10). 5) çakāracakāravargayo*h* (iv., 4).

Taittirīyaprātiçākhya. 1) a-kāra (i., 21); i-kāra (ii., 28); hakāra (i., 13); a-varṇa (vii., 5); i-varṇa, etc. (x., 4). 3) pa (iv., 30); na (iv., 32); xa (ix., 3); ta, ṭa (vii., 13); ṭha, tha (vii., 14); ra (i., 19). 4) repha (i., 19). 5) kavarga (ii., 35); cavarga (ii., 36); ṭavarga (xiv., 20). Here, also, all these terms are regularly inflected.

Kātyāyanīyaprātiçākhya. 1) ai-kāra, au-kāra (i., 73); lr̥i-kāra (i., 87); i-varṇa (i., 116). 2) uvoshppā*h* (i., 70); a- (i., 71). 3) ra (i., 40); nu*h* (iii., 132); this last stands for n. 4) repha (i., 40). 5) tavarga (iii., 92).

This Prātiçākhya has also Pāṇini's et etc. which must be an interpolation; all these terms are regularly inflected[1].

Atharvaprātiçākhya. 1) akāra (i., 36); lr̥ikāra (i., 4); lakāra (i., 5); shakāra (i., 23); r̥ivarṇa (i., 37). 3) ya, ra (i., 68) ça-sha-s-eshu (ii., 6). 4) repha (i., 28). 5) cavarga (i., 7); ṭavargīye (ii., 12); caṭavargaya*h* (ii., 14). Here these terms are also treated as in the other Prātiçākhyas.

Yāska has u-kāra (p. 32).

It is in this way that the Kātantra treats the alphabetic sounds: 1) e-kāra (i., 2, 6); ça-kāra (i., 4, 3); u-varṇa (i., 2, 3); r̥i-varṇa (i., 2, 4). 2) e (i., 2, 2); e ay (i., 2, 12). 3) na*h* (i., 4, 8) ra-prakr̥iti (i., 5, 14); re (i., 5, 17); ram (i., 2, 10); lam (i., 2, 11); cam (i., 4, 6); çi (or ? çe, cfr. i., 5, 6; i., 4, 13). 4) visarjanīya etc. 5) lacaṭavarga (i., 4, 5); ṭavarga, tavarga (ii., 4, 46); ka- pavarga (ii., 5, 29). Thus the inflectional treatment is here the same as in the other works already mentioned, and as in them, we here also find compounds, *e. g.* yaralavā*h* (i., 1, 14), ṅañaṇanamā*h* (i., 1, 13), etc.

In some instances the Kātantra has the Pāṇinīyan -t; *e.g.* et, ot.

By Pāṇini's system, 1) letters affected in a similar way are collectively indicated by pratyāhāras formed out of the Çivasūtras, and these are

---

1) See above p. 27.

2) These terms also figure as parts of samāsa compounds: Sa-yam īkāram (R̥igv. pr. xiv., 15); kakhapa-kāra (Taitt. pr. viii., 23); sa-lakāra (Ath. pr. i., 39); r̥i-shkkau (Kāt. pr. i., 65); a-cañau (do. i., 85); sa-ya-va*h* (do. i., 111).

inflected like ordinary nouns ending in consonants[1], and they even form parts of samāsa compounds[2]. Again 2) to express a class of letters which are phonetically allied (varga) the letter -u is affixed to the first of the class, and the words thus formed are inflected like ordinary nouns in -u, and are also combined in samāsa[3]. Lastly to indicate special letters, Pāṇini uses *A.*, for vowels: 1) the vowel followed by -t[4]; 2) the vowel itself[5]; in both cases inflection is allowed. *B.*, for consonants: 1) the consonant followed by -a which word is then inflected[6]; 2) by a special name, *e.g.* ru (r)[7].

The use of all these several ways of referring to letters is precise, and has in each case a clearly defined purpose.

Thus if it is necessary to specially define a vowel, -t is added according to the sūtra—"taparas tatkālasya" (i., 1, 70). If the short vowel-sound is itself used, this is to include the analogous modifications. If a vowel is given with -t, it excludes all but what is actually written. Such conciseness is unknown to the earlier books. By Ṛigvedapr. i., 13 the short vowel also includes the long. Abstract nouns (*e.g.* etva) are formed from letters even in the Prātiçākhyas.

II. Analogous to the pratyāhāras are the symbols used by Pāṇini and treated by him in the same way. Thus we find them inflected[8], and combined in samāsa[9] just like real words.

And in some cases, such terms are still more compressed, several being formed into one[10].

Terminations are also inflected like real words. It is possible that this practice, as regards terminations at least, is older than Pāṇini[11].

---

1) *e.g.* ikaḥ (gen. s.) i., 1, 3; halaḥ (nom. pl.) i., 1, 7; aj-jhalau (dual nom.) i., 1, 10; acaḥ (gen. s.) i., 1, 48; yaṇaḥ (do.) i., 1, 45; alaḥ (do.) i., 1, 52; acaḥ (i., 1, 57); aci (i., 1, 59); acām (i., 1, 73).

2) *e.g.* ekāl—i., 2, 41. ekāc, i., 1, 14. In all cases the rules relating to the use of the plural and dual are accurately observed where such words are in samāsa.

3) *e.g.* cuṭū—1, 3, 7.

4) *e.g.* īdūtau—i., 1, 19.

5) *e.g.* of ṛi, uḥ (gen. sing.) i., 1, 51 etc.; vy-upadhaḥ (i., 2, 26); a a (viii., 4, 68); ai (iii., 4, 90).

6) maḥ (viii., 3, 23); māt (i., 1, 12); ra-para (i., 1, 51); naḥ and ṇaḥ (viii., 4, 1); ra-shābhyām (do.).

7) viii., 2, 66 etc.

8) *e.g.* jas-i (i., 1, 32); itā (i., 1, 71); ṅiṭudavaḥ (i., 3, 5); liṅgaḥ (iii., 4, 102); leṭaḥ (iii., 4, 94). This is done with pure symbols, and also with symbols composed of a termination etc. with anubandhas.

9) *e.g.* lukçlulup-aḥ (i., 1, 61).

10) kkṅit-i (i., 1, 5).

11) *e.g.* Bhir-bhyām-para (Taitt. pr. viii., 14). Rau-dvivacanānta (Ath. pr. ii., 47).

Symbolic terms appear to have been nearly all invented by Pāṇini; but few occur in treatises of the older school, and there as interpolations. Such being the case, they are inflected as in Pāṇini's Grammar.

The symbols used in the **Kātantra** are inflected in exactly the same way[1].

III. It is possible to trace the gradual separation of **roots** from the words in which they appear, as the Brāhmaṇas, which are unquestionably older (except perhaps the Gopathabrāhmaṇa) than any grammatical treatises that we possess, frequently discuss the etymology of words. I have already[2] given some specimens of these primitive attempts; they do not follow any regular system, but nevertheless show that roots were even then clearly distinguished.

Roots (in the ordinary sense of the word) are not given in the Nighaṇṭus, but verbs are nearly always given in the third person of the present tense, and are classified according to meaning[3]. Yāska terms these forms dhātu; but he, again, by no means follows any uniform system. For the most part he gives the third person to express the root[4], but sometimes he uses a verbal noun for the same purpose[5]. There can be no doubt, however, that he fully recognised the identity of the root though it appears in various forms in some cases. Thus (Naig. ii., 1—p. 40) he says: "Tad yeshu padeshu svarasa*m*skārau samarthau prādeçikena guṇenā 'nvitau syātā*m* tathā tāni nirbrūyād; athā 'nanvite 'rthe 'prādeçike vikāre 'rthanitya*h* parīxeta kenacid vṛittisāmānyenā, 'vidyamāne sāmānye 'py axaravarṇasāmānyān nirbrūyān; na tv eva na nirbrūyān. Na sa*m*skāram ādriyeta, viçayavatyo hi vṛittayo bhavanti. Yathārtha*m* vibhakti*h* sa*m*namayet: prattam avattam iti dhātvādī eva çishyete. Athā 'py aster nivṛittisthāneshv ādilopo bhavati: sta*h* santī 'ty. Athā 'py antalopo bhavati: gatvā gatam ity. Athā 'py upadhālopo bhavati: jagmatur jagmur ity. Athā 'py upadhāvikāro bhavati: rājā daṇḍī 'ty. Athā 'pi varṇalopo bhavati: tat tvā yāmī 'ty. Athā 'pi dvivarṇalopas: tṛica ity. Athā 'py ādiviparyayo bhavati: jyotir ghano bindur vāṭya ity. Athā 'py ādyantaviparyayo bhavati: stokā rajju*h* sikatās tarkv iti." This

---

1) *e.g.* dhuṭ (ii., 1, 13); dhuṭi (ii., 1, 19); jasçasau (ii., 1, 4); jasi (ii., 1, 15); si*h* (ii., 1, 5); ṅi*h* (ii., 1, 27). In a very few instances there is no inflection expressed.

2) Above p. 27.

3) ii., 6, 14. 18. 19; iii., 14. 20. 21. 22. etc. cfr. Naig. p. 55 ffg.

4) *e. g.* çaknote*h* (p. 32); ma*m*hate*h* (p. 33); hante*h* (do.); kashate*h* (p. 40), etc. Hundreds of examples could be given.

5) See *e.g.* the various etymologies of Nighaṇṭu (on p. 31).

passage and the following lines show clearly how far Pāṇini's great predecessor had got in matter of technical system.

Yāska inflects the third person sing. pres. par. in just the same way as the author of the Prātiçākhyas, as I shall now show.

The Ṛigveda-prātiçākhya has both grammatical roots (*e. g.* vṛitu)[1] and also the third person singular of the present again inflected or turned into a noun, which serves the same purpose—dhātor bibheter jayater niyaç ca[2]. In this last instance the two first-mentioned roots are given in this way, as is most commonly done, in this Prātiçākhya, and the last only is given in what is now the usual form.

The Taittirīya pr. gives roots in a single instance 'cha-khi-bhujeshu'[3]; in the Kātyāyana pr. there are many instances: *a*) where roots have an inflectional -a, -i, or -u added, *e. g.* sade (iii., 48), vṛidha (iii., 112), sahe*h* (iii., 121), çase*h* (iii., 122), ruhau (iv., 44), vāhau (iii., 44), vā*m*sau (v., 11); *b*) where the consonant ending is left unaltered—vṛidhavṛijo*h* (iii., 112), styāstano*h* (iii., 68), anindho*h* (v., 33); *c*) where the third person (sing. pres. par.) is again inflected: pātau (iii., 27), siṅcatau (iii., 45), sīdate*h* (iii., 58), etc.[4]

The Atharva-prātiçākhya agrees in this respect with Kātyāyanaprātiçākhya; we find in it—with -a: kṛipe (i., 64),—with i: hani-gamyo*h* (i., 86), vide*h* (i., 90),—with the natural final consonant: çān-mān-dān-ām (i., 87). There are also instances of the third pers. sing. present par. inflected: rājatau (ii., 36), a-jahāte*h* (ii., 46).

In the Kātantra we find both 1) the third person sing. pres. par. as well as 2) roots, both used for the same purposes, *e. g.* 1) karote*h* (ii., 4, 49); 2) *e. g.* gup, tij, kit (iii., 2, 2); mān, badh, dān, çān (iii., 2, 3), curādi (iii., 2, 11), bhī-hrī-bhṛi-huv-ām (iii., 2, 21). It will be observed that all the forms of roots noticed as yet are what may be termed natural and are such as would be easily noticed from their use as adjectives etc.

Pāṇini's treatment of these roots is not quite consistent, but he uses 1) the old forms (3rd pers. sing. pres. par.) in only a few instances; in all the remaining cases—an immense number—he uses 2) roots and special forms, or—and this is an improvement of his own—3) in dhātupāṭha forms, or with indicatory letters added. For example: 1) indhi-bha-

1) ix., 2.

2) xiv., 16.

3) xiv., 8.

4) "Ind. Studien," iv., pp. 91-2.

vati-bhyām (i., 2, 6); ety-edhaty-ūṭh-su (vi., 1, 89); and inflected—eter liṅgi (vii., 4, 24). 2) To these he adds vowels to facilitate inflection— *a.*—Mṛiḍa-mṛida-gudha-kusha-kliça-vada-vas-a*h* (i., 2, 7). *i.*—grahi, svapi (i., 2, 8); gami, sṛicchi (i., 3, 29). *u.*—ūrṇu (i., 2, 3). In svid etc. (i., 2, 19) the natural consonant ending is left, and in dī-dhī-ve-vīt-ām (i., 1, 6) the roots are in their natural form. 3) *e.g.* çīṅ (i., 2, 19); pūṅ (i., 2, 22). But the roots are seldom in their dhātupāṭha forms: *e.g.* sthā is usually put, and not shṭhā. Such roots are all inflected: *e.g.* da*h* (from √dā) in i., 3, 20; je*h* from √ji (i., 3, 19); bruva*h* (vii., 3, 93) from √brū.

It thus appears that before Pāṇini the grammarians understood by dhātu: 1) parts of the verb, especially the third person singular present parasmaipada which seems to be the form earliest thus used technically, and 2) natural roots. Pāṇini finally added roots such as we find in the dhātupāṭha. The Uṇādi sūtras follow the same system as Pāṇini in every way.

IV. The grammarians also inflect words already inflected or words which are naturally uninflected; and this appears in the earliest treatises, *e.g.* the Prātiçākhyas. The most common instance is the use of the third person singular of the present tense of verbs as already described[1]; next come inflections of indeclinable words—particles and prepositions.

In the Taittirīya pr. we find āy-am (ix., 14), āv-am (ix., 15), ar-am (x., 8), and ār-am (x., 9) as inflections of the sounds āy etc., but this prātiçākhya generally gives concrete examples, and these are not treated by inflection.

The Kātyāyana- and Atharva-prātiçākhyas furnish many more examples. In the former we find: dyave*h*, as genitive of dyavi (iii., 67); stuvantyām, as locative of stuvantī (iii., 70); teshu, as loc. plur. of te (iii., 119); ne*h*, as gen. of ni (iii., 58); kṛidhau, as loc. of kṛidhi (iii., 32); tataxau (iii., 69); vājayanteshu (iii., 98) etc., and even some words are left uninflected.

In the latter we find: shaṭ-puras-o*h* (i., 63); īyas-a*h* (i., 89); pu*m*sa*h*- *i.e.* of the word pu*m*s (i., 81). Pāṇini (viii., 3, 6) has puma*h*.

The Kātantra occasionally furnishes words with a secondary inflection (*e.g.* ala*m*-khalv-o*h* (last section, 1).

Pāṇini, however, carried this practice to a surprising extent; with him, every kind of word, real or artificial, inflected already or not in-

1) This is even done by the mediæval commentators occasionally.

flected, everything is capable of inflection. Thus *e. g.* āṅa*h* (i., 3, 28); sama*h* (i., 3, 29); itau (i., 1, 16); taraptamapau (i., 1, 22); asmado (i., 2, 59); ne*h* (i., 3, 17); parivyavebhya*h* (i., 3, 18); adhe*h* (i., 3, 33); adaso (i., 1, 12); çe (i., 1, 13); uṅa*h* (i., 1, 17) etc.

There is a curious circumstance connected with this grammar of artificial words as developed by the Indian grammarians—the use of gender as applied to these terms. It seems arbitrary—being masculine apparently—not neuter as one would expect.

As will have been noticed in some of the above examples, the rules of sandhi are often neglected in the case of grammatical fictions, and this course is obviously necessary to preserve the integrity of the symbols in question. Thus we find uṇādi where we should expect uṇṇādi, and the declension of such words as end in -s or a consonant is necessarily somewhat irregular. The Çākaṭāyanavyākaraṇa displays more such irregularities than Pāṇini.

The technical syntax of the grammatical technical language is also an important subject; as I have already remarked (p. 43), it appears to have been almost created by Pāṇini. The sūtras which regulate this part of his technical system are i., 1, 49-50, 66 and 67. The Çākaṭāyanavyākaraṇa follows much the same system (i., 1, 57-60); but, apparently, in order to make the sūtras more concise we here find a new irregularity, and compound words are always in the singular number.

There is very little of this in the Aindra treatises. The Ṛigvedaprātiçākhya (i., 14) gives one such rule ("asāv amum iti tadbhāvam uktam") by which the letter to be changed is put in the nominative and the resulting letter in the accusative. This is done in the Kātantra, Kātyāyanīya pr. (iii., 6-7 etc.) and Taittirīya pr. (*e. g.* v., 20). Pāṇini, on the other hand, puts the letter to be changed in the genitive, and the result in the nominative, in which the Atharva pr. (*e. g.* iii., 44) mostly concurs, though the older system is sometimes used also (*e. g.* iii., 46 and 52). A comparison of the rules in the Kātantra and Pāṇini, by which i, u, etc. before a etc. become y, v, etc., will make this very plain. In Pāṇini (vi., 1, 77) the rule simply is: "iko yaṇ aci". In the Kātantra four rules (i., 2, 8-11) are found: "ivarṇo yam"....; "vam uvarṇa*h*"; "ram ṛivarṇa*h*"; "lam lṛivarṇa*h*". In both cases it is obvious that this technical syntax has arisen out of abbreviations. Thus in the first the full sentence would be: "ika*h* (sthāne) yaṇ aci (pare)[1]". In the last it would be:

1) Such a complete expression occurs in the Ṛigv. pr. *e. g.* xiv., 15.

"ivarṇo yam (āpadyate)". This use of the locative case seems to be as early as that of the accusative, for it occurs in the Ṛigvedaprātiçākhya and in the other similar works; but Pāṇini's rule (i,, 1, 66) gives it a precise meaning, and fits it into his system.

The above will give some slight idea of the numerous problems which yet remain to be worked out in respect of Indian Grammar; some of these, such as the history of the notion of 'vikaraṇa', are of great interest, but I must leave them for the present.

END

Additions and Corrections.

Page:	*Line:*	
6	14	*For:* third section *read:* second section
"	22	" Aindri " Aindrī
"	*note* 4	*Add:* Profr. Weber ("Ind. Studien" xiii., p. 335) points out a passage much like this in the Taitt. S. vi., 4. 7. 3. The only C. now accessible to me—that by Bhaṭṭa Bhāskara—throws no light on this passage as far as my present object is concerned.
8	2	*For:* such a book *read:* such a book or books
9	28	" Kaccāyanappakaraṅae " Kaccāyanappakaraṇae
10	2	" Eḻuttaδiγāram " Ĕḻuttaδiγāram
12	14	*Add:* uriššōl is probably a translation of guṇavacana, a term that is used in the Çabdamaṇidarpaṇa (Canarese).
13	33	*For:* upsarga *read:* upasarga
"	40	" laxanā " laxaṇa
15	32	" kāṇ " -kān
16	2	*Add:* The M. Bhāshya (Benares ed. p. 7, *b.*) has three sthānas.
"	*note* 10	" saptamī occurs in Yāska (p. 37) etc.
"	" 11	" cfr. M. Bhāshya, f. 9 *b.*
17	9	*For:* viṇai *read:* vinai
"	*after* 23	*Add:* The Tamiḻ has iḍam 'place' for person; so we find (in Yāska etc.) sthāna used with the same meaning.
"	*note* 5	*Read:* bhūta-bhavishyad-vartamānā*h*.
19	*note*	Lṅiga Liṅga
23	8	*Add:* Yāska uses upadhā in the original sense (p. 40).
"	18	*For:* older *read:* oldest
25	*note* 2, *line* 7	" °rūpāni " °rūpāṇi
26	*note, line* 8	" udac " udaṅc
27	13	" çixukā*h* " çixakā*h*
"	22	" oshṭya° " oshṭhya°
"	28	" nāmam " nāman
28	*note* 2	" Siddānta° " Siddhānta°
29	14	" au ār " au āv
32		*Add:* N. *after* Gārgya; *for* Macakīya *read* Mācakīya
35	4-5	*For:* which are anterior to *read:* some of which are probably anterior to
40	*note* 3	*Add:* India Office ed. p. 1872 (vol. iii.).
44	21	The Indian accounts of Pāṇini (as of many other famous men in Sanskrit literary history) closely resemble the mediæval notions of Vergil's life.
45	19	*For:* have *read:* leave
47	14	" Prātiçākyas " Prātiçākhyas
48	16	" Rigveda° " Ṛigveda°
49	21	*Add:* There is another C. by Annambhaṭṭa; see "Ind. Studien" iv., p. 332.
52	21	*For:* Caitrukuṭī *read:* Caitrakuṭī

Page:	*Line*:	
65		*Add:* It should be remarked that it was a fortunate circumstance that the Sanskrit Grammar could be, more or less, applied to agglutinative or monosyllabic languages; had Sanskrit been of the Semitic type, this important instrument of progress would have remained useless.
75	18	*Add:* Clerical errors often seriously alter proper names (see Féer's "Études Bouddhiques" p. 373 of the "*Journal Asiatique*" vol. v. of Series vii.); palæography, only, can here demonstrate the true reading.
78	29	*For:* bhujayān *read:* bhujaṅgān
81	31	" Vetālapañcavimçatī, Çukasaptatī " °vimçati, °saptati
87	11	*Add:* I should have added 'san' (i., 86) which is also used by Pāṇini as a name of the desiderative (ii., 4, 47; vi., 4, 16 etc.) as Profr. Whitney remarks in his commentary on this sūtra.
"	33	*For:* *a.* *read:* *e.*
92	18	though his excellent though this excellent
95	5	*Add:* The words in ( ) are additions of the Grantha text; the Nāgarī text has only "vṛiçcikṛishyoḥ kikan".
98	27	*For:* (i., 1) *and* (i., 2) *read:* (i., 1, 11) *and* (i., 3, 11)
100	3	" nearly " merely
103	19-20	" A. D. " B. C.
109	17	" grammars " grammarians

As on former occasions, I must urge as my apology for misprints, irregularities of transcription and other errors, the circumstances that I am several hundred miles away from the Press (communication with which is very slow), and that what I do, is done under constant interruptions of every possible kind.

I hope that I have not left uncorrected any serious error likely to embarrass my readers.